THE
POCKET BIBLE
SERIES

The Allotment Pocket Bible

The Baking Pocket Bible

The Camping Pocket Bible

The Cat Lover's Pocket Bible

The Christmas Pocket Bible

The Cook's Pocket Bible

The Cricket Pocket Bible

The Dad's Pocket Bible

The DIY Pocket Bible

The Dog Lover's Pocket Bible

The Football Pocket Bible

The Gardener's Pocket Bible

The Golf Pocket Bible

The Jane Austen Pocket Bible

The Knitting Pocket Bible

The London Pocket Bible

The Mum's Pocket Bible

The Outdoor Pocket Bible

The Pregnancy Pocket Bible

The Railway Pocket Bible

The Traveller's Pocket Bible

The Wedding Pocket Bible

The Wine Pocket Bible

THE
**ALLOTMENT
POCKET BIBLE**

THE
ALLOTMENT
POCKET BIBLE

EMMA COOPER

This edition first published in Great Britain 2011 by
Crimson Publishing, a division of Crimson Business Ltd
Westminster House
Kew Road
Richmond
Surrey
TW9 2ND

A catalogue record for this book is available from the British Library.

ISBN 978 1 907087 219

Typeset by IDSUK (DataConnection) Ltd
Printed and bound by Lego Print SpA, Trento

CONTENTS

INTRODUCTION

In our health and environmentally conscious age, the latest 'must have' is an allotment where you can grow your own fruit and vegetables, or a few kitchen herbs and some flowers to help support the local wildlife. British people love allotments because they allow us to get involved in two of our favourite pastimes – gardening and queuing (as many allotment sites now have long waiting lists!).

The Allotment Pocket Bible offers light-hearted, yet down-to-earth, advice on maintaining and planning an allotment and information to help you to grow your own fruit and vegetables. If you're a novice gardener, you'll discover why so many people are flocking to allotments, and the joys of growing your own. It also tackles the thorny problem of finding and choosing your plot, whether you're looking for a large allotment or just a quiet corner in which to sow your seeds.

For those with a little more experience, you'll find advice on what to grow and when, and how to store your seeds and your produce. There's guidance on how to organise and manage your plot, and a few tasty recipes to make the most of your harvest.

There's also a quick peek at the history of allotments, and modern allotment communities, and information on how to get your children safely involved with growing (and eating!) their vegetables.

The growing calendar at the back of the book is a useful tool for planning your garden every year. Together with plenty of advice and tips, and the Glossary at the end of the book, it will get you off to a flying start, and in no time you'll have all you need to make growing your own an enjoyable part of your life for years to come.

ALL ABOUT ALLOTMENTS: BENEFITS AND COMMUNITIES

Allotments are a quintessential part of the British landscape. Their purpose is to make land available to anyone on which they can grow food crops, but allotments have come to mean much more than that to those who tend them. In this chapter we take a look back at how they have developed throughout history, examine the benefits of having an allotment and explore the communities which have grown up around allotments.

♛ THE DEVELOPMENT OF ♛ THE ALLOTMENT

- **AD410**: In Saxon times communities cleared land together, sharing out 'allotted' areas between themselves.

- **1066**: Following the Norman conquest, land ownership was increasingly confined to lords of the manor and the church.

- **1600**: During the reign of Elizabeth I the first mention of allotments is made, as land is given to the poor to compensate them for the enclosure of previously common land.

- **1845**: The General Enclosure Act included a requirement to provide land for allotments where common land was enclosed.

- **1887**: The Allotments and Cottage Gardens Compensation for Crops Act obliged local authorities to provide allotments, if there was a demand for them.

- **1907**: The Smallholdings and Allotment Act clarified the responsibilities of local authorities to provide allotments.

- **1914**: Germany's blockade during the First World War led to an increased demand for allotments, although it fell again after the war.

- **1939**: The Second World War, and its Dig For Victory campaign, brought allotments and kitchen gardens to the forefront of British life. The number of allotments in the UK peaked at 1.5 million.

- **1960**: Disuse and development led to a large decrease in the number of allotments available.

- **1975**: An interest in self-sufficiency, and the popular television show *The Good Life* caused a resurgence in interest in allotments during the 1970s.

- **2002**: Organic vegetable growing got a big boost when Monty Don took over as the main presenter on *Gardeners' World*.

Pocket Fact

The Victorians used allotments to encourage temperance in the working classes – a man productively employed feeding his family spent less time in the pub!

MODERN RESURGENCE

Despite increased interest in the idea of 'self-sufficiency' during the 1970s, the post-war years showed a marked decline in the use of allotments and as many allotments were sold off for development, or fell into disuse, the number of plots available plummeted.

However, concerns about our impact on the environment, and regular food scares, have encouraged a modern allotment resurgence, with many more people determined to 'grow their own'. The new 'allotmenteer' is younger, and far more likely to be female, than in times gone by.

Pocket Fact 🥄

In 2006 the Allotments Regeneration Initiative said that women were the fastest-growing group of allotment holders, renting around 59,000 plots.

Modern allotment and kitchen gardeners have found support from celebrity chefs, many of whom are happy to get their hands dirty in search of fresh, organic produce. Local organisations, such as Incredible Edible Todmorden (www.incredible-edible-todmorden.co.uk) are encouraging residents to grow as much of their own food as they can, on any spare land they can find, and even children are getting started growing their own, with a number of local and national campaigns supporting the development of school vegetable gardens.

Pocket Fact 🥄

Since 2007 sales of vegetable seeds have soared, and in 2009 70% of seeds sold were for vegetables.

♛ ALLOTMENT BENEFITS ♛

There's no doubt about it, allotments are making a comeback. Growing your own fruit and vegetables not only provides you with fresh, seasonal produce, it also brings a multitude of other benefits.

HEALTH

- Five-a-day: it's much more enticing to eat vegetables when you've grown them yourself, and that's particularly true for children.

- Growing your own gives you easy access to organically grown, chemical-free produce.

- Gardening doesn't have to be hard work, but you'll be getting plenty of exercise in the fresh air.
- Green spaces have been proven to be good for our mental health.
- There's scientific evidence that simply getting your hands in the soil can make you happier!

Pocket Fact 🔨

The PlantforLife campaign (www.plantforlife.info) recommends we all spend at least 20 minutes a day (or two hours a week) gardening or otherwise enjoying green spaces.

ECONOMIC

- The rent on an allotment is a mere fraction of the cost of a year's fruit and vegetables, so you can save money by growing your own.
- You can also save money by ditching your gym membership, and getting your exercise outdoors instead.
- Allotments are a cheap source of recreation and entertainment for families – many kids love playing in the dirt!

Pocket Fact 🔨

In 2010 a British man grew £700 of fruit and vegetables on his balcony and windowsills.

ENVIRONMENTAL

- Green spaces produce fresh air, and are an important part of urban life.
- You can grow your own without resorting to the environmentally damaging chemical pesticides and fertilisers commonly used in agriculture.

- Home-grown produce has no food miles, saving on fossil fuel use and greenhouse gas emissions.

- Buying less food saves on packaging waste, and a compost heap makes use of your vegetable waste rather than sending it off to landfill.

- Allotments and gardens are valuable wildlife habitats.

Pocket Fact 🍳

Research published in 2010 showed that honeybees have a far more varied diet in cities than they do in the countryside.

♕ ALLOTMENT COMMUNITIES ♕

If your plot is on an allotment site or other communal project then you'll have access to all the benefits of being part of a community.

Some allotment sites are still run by the local authority, while others are managed by an allotment association. Each one is different in terms of the facilities it offers and the strength of the community spirit.

Pocket Tip 🐝

Spend enough time investigating local allotment sites to find one with a welcoming community. Many allotment sites have web-sites to publicise their events and encourage local participation.

On traditionally run allotment sites you may find yourself surrounded by experienced gardeners who are more than willing to show you the ropes, offer help and advice and share spare seeds and plants throughout the year.

Pocket Tip 🦤

If you have a choice of plots on offer, chat to your potential neighbours — they'll be able to help you choose the best one.

The modern trend is towards vibrant allotment communities that offer an on-site shop, toilets, shared tools and community events and shows. If there's space, your site may also have plots set aside for wildlife gardens, or offer space to school gardens and gardening therapy projects.

ENCOURAGING COMMUNITY

Here are some ideas for fostering community spirit on your allotment site:

- Make your allotment site kid-friendly, with safe play areas and picnic spots.

- Offer a vacant plot to your local school, for a gardening club.

- Host shared meals. If you don't have any cooking facilities then you can encourage picnics, barbecues and 'pot lucks', where people bring food to share.

- Organise seed and plant swaps in spring, so people can exchange spares for something new.

- A winter lecture series, with visiting speakers, is a great way to keep gardeners interested during the 'off' season.

- Arrange group visits to gardens that are open to the public, or open your allotment site to visitors via the National Gardens Scheme (NGS).

- Hold an allotment show, or 'giant vegetable' competitions. A contest to see who can grow the tallest sunflower is popular with children.

- Open your site to the public once or twice a year, to show off your hard work. 'Apple Day' is a popular choice, with activities from apple bobbing to apple pressing, or you can have a harvest festival.

ANTI-SOCIAL BEHAVIOUR

Although allotmenteers are generally helpful and generous people, public allotment sites can be vulnerable to theft and vandalism. Make sure you're aware of the security arrangements and ask for advice on keeping your patch secure. Your local police force will be able to advise you on plot security issues, but here are some tips to bear in mind.

- On a site level, good fences greatly help security. If money is tight then a thick hedge (of spiny plants) may be cheaper and more effective once it matures.

- Encouraging community participation in allotment activities and events will cut down on vandalism.

- Don't leave your tools lying around: put them away or take them home. You could try burying a tool store in a corner of the plot.

- Sheds are often targeted by thieves; leaving them unlocked may save on damage.

- Encourage plotholders to mark their property, so it can be recovered if it is stolen.

- DIY garden structures are cheaper and easier to repair if they are damaged.

In the event that there are problems on your allotment site with anti-social behaviour, the key to solving them is to discuss the issues and potential solutions as a group. Usually a 'Blitz spirit' emerges, with everyone pulling together to help repair the damage.

If improvements need to be made to security then your allotment association can bring those up with the allotment officer on the local council.

Pocket Fact

The Queen herself is an allotmenteer: a vegetable patch was installed in the grounds of Buckingham Palace in 2009.

2

TYPES OF ALLOTMENT

Officially there are three different types of allotment: permanent, temporary and privately owned. Permanent allotments cannot be sold, or used for a different purpose, without the consent of the Secretary of State. Temporary allotment sites are usually owned by the local authorities, but don't have the same protection and can therefore be sold. You will also find sites on private land.

These official categories don't do much to describe the features of an allotment though, or help allotmenteers to plan their crops. In addition to these official allotment categories, it can help to identify allotments by their location – namely urban, country-side, garden or even shared land – as these different locations all have different features and requirements. This chapter will take a look at these different types of allotment, the areas they can be found in, and how to decide which type is best for you.

♛ URBAN ♛

WHERE THEY'RE FOUND

The word 'allotment' brings to mind a large plot of ground, intended for growing vegetables, on a site where lots of plots are arranged neatly together. You may imagine a quiet and peaceful spot, surrounded by hedges and trees, but the reality is often very different. Urban allotment sites are generally in the middle of towns, or on the outskirts. They're often next to main roads, or in the middle of housing estates. They may be in corners that have resisted development for decades.

Urban allotments tend to incorporate all of the typical features you associate with allotments, and so can serve as a useful guide for any type of allotment.

TYPICAL LAYOUT AND FEATURES

A traditional allotment is a rectangle of ground that measures 10 rods: an esoteric measurement that is the equivalent of around 300 square yards, 2,700 square feet, 250 square metres or $\frac{1}{16}$ of an acre. To put it another way, it's roughly the size of the penalty box on a football field.

However, the size and shape of plots varies widely, particularly now that waiting lists are increasing and plots are being divided up into smaller shares so that more people can have access to the land. It's always best to ask about the exact size rather than making any assumptions.

Pocket Tip

If a whole allotment sounds too big for you to take on, you may be able to rent a half or quarter plot, or find a friend to share with.

The features on an allotment site may include the following.

● **A shed**. Sheds are allowed on some sites, but not others. You may even be lucky enough to inherit an old one. Many plotholders put their own together from scrap materials, but always check if you're allowed one before you start building.

● **Access to water**. There are usually taps at regular intervals between plots.

● **Boundaries**. Some sites mark the boundaries of plots in particular ways, while others expect you to do your own.

● **Paths**. Grass paths are common between plots; gravel elsewhere. It's unusual for even the entry road to be paved.

● **Gates**. Access gates are often locked to prevent problems with theft and vandalism – if so, you will be issued with a key.

You may also find separate interior gates in fences aimed to keep rabbits out.

A few sites provide toilets and some even have a permanent shop or club house.

Pocket Tip 🛒

On some allotment sites, the water pressure may depend on how far you are from the water main, so it's worth checking that any potential plots have a reasonable supply.

Some useful scrap materials for use on an allotment

- *Pallets are easy to come by and a useful source of wood for building raised beds or even sheds.*
- *If a neighbour is having their windows changed, ask if you can have the old ones. They're great for making cold frames (see p. 50). Local window firms may even have a skip you can rifle through – but do ask first!*
- *Recycle old bricks into hard-wearing paths. You may also be able to find some old paving slabs.*
- *Unwanted net curtains are very good at keeping the birds off your crops, as is a scarecrow wearing your old clothes.*
- *Plastic barrels are great for water butts, but do make sure they weren't used for something toxic, and give them a good wash before use.*

RULES AND REGULATIONS

The *raison d'être* of allotment sites is to provide land for growing food, and when you sign up you should be presented with the rules and regulations. Many sites have their own 'bylaws' that you must abide by to keep your plot, but there are some common rules:

- It is usually prohibited to sell any of the produce that you grow.

- If you don't keep your plot 'in good order' (standards vary!) then you will lose it.

- Permanent structures, and even trees, may not be allowed.

- Some sites allow 'livestock', while others don't. Even where chickens are accepted you may find that bees are not allowed, as people are often afraid of being stung.

- Dogs may or may not be allowed.

- Unsupervised children may be also be an issue, particularly where there are vandalism problems.

- Bonfires may be restricted or banned entirely.

Pocket Tip 🐦
Always check your allotment agreement to see what is allowed, and ask if you're unsure.

WHAT IS GROWN AND WHAT GROWS BEST

A whole allotment is a large space that allows you to grow almost anything you want. Many growers devote their plot to staple crops that take up a lot of space but need little management, and an allotment is ideal for those. Others treat their space as though it were a garden, with a mix of plants and flowers. Be wary of investing too much in perennial plants and trees, particularly at first. They are hard to move if you decide to give up your plot, or if the plot is taken from you – an inherent risk associated with gardening on land you do not own.

Pumpkins and winter squashes (which store through the autumn) are great on allotments as they are large plants, and good at suppressing weeds. Courgettes are more problematic, as they ripen and grow too large very quickly. Most families can make good use of a lot of potatoes, which are easy to grow and take care of themselves. Hardy winter vegetables such as Brussels sprouts and kale will take care of themselves on unpleasant winter days, when you'd rather stay at home!

♛ COUNTRYSIDE ♛

WHERE THEY'RE FOUND

It is not uncommon for farmers to section off an underused field to rent out as allotments. Although farms are usually a way out into the countryside, a few are on the peripheries of towns and villages. You may also have a National Trust property in your local area which hosts allotments, or be close to allotments on land owned by Network Rail or British Waterways.

Useful websites to search for allotments

- *DirectGov lists the main local authorities, with their contact details (www.direct.gov.uk/en/HomeAndCommunity/ YourlocalcouncilandCouncilTax/YourCommunity/ DG_4018786).*
- *The National Society of Allotment and Leisure Gardeners (www.nsalg.org.uk) can help you find a plot, as can the Scottish Allotments and Gardens Society (www.sags.org.uk) in Scotland.*
- *The National Trust is making allotments available through the Landshare (www.landshare.net) scheme, which is a great place to look for available sites.*
- *The Federation of City Farms and Community Gardens (www.farmgarden.org.uk) can advise you on community schemes in your local area.*
- *Contact Network Rail (www.networkrail.co.uk) for information on renting nearby land, and check the Waterscape website (www.waterscape.com) for information on leisure activities near British waterways.*

TYPICAL LAYOUT AND FEATURES

Where allotments are provided on privately owned land, rather than by councils, the size and shape of plots is less well defined. On a farm you may be able to choose how much land you want; in more unusual locations such as National Trust plots it's hard to predict what sort of facilities will be on offer.

A farm may provide large quantities of animal manure to use as fertiliser, or spoiled hay for mulching, and there's the potential to collect unwanted scrap for reuse (agricultural plastic sheeting, or old railway sleepers). This will depend on the individual nature of the plot.

RULES AND REGULATIONS

Again, the rules and regulations will depend on the type of site and your landlord. An allotment on a farm may come with a similar set of restrictions to a publicly owned allotment site, or none.

WHAT IS GROWN AND WHAT GROWS BEST

The types of crops that you can grow, and which grow best, will be very similar to those for more urban allotments, so have a look back at p.11 for ideas.

If your plot is a fair distance from your home then stick to crops that take care of themselves for much of the time – pumpkins and squashes, and potatoes, are ideal. Cabbages and other members of the brassica family are also a good bet, provided you give them enough protection from the local wildlife!

♚ GARDEN ♚

WHERE THEY'RE FOUND

Your home may have a front or back garden you could put to good use. However, in our age of increased urbanisation and land-grabbing, many homes these days don't have much in the way of a garden. This doesn't mean you can't join in the allotment movement though. There may be shared spaces nearby (see p.15 for more information on shared plots). Blocks of flats may have balconies and fire escapes, or even a roof garden, but even a windowsill will get your gardening off to a good start.

TYPICAL LAYOUT AND FEATURES

If you're gardening on your own property, you will already be familiar with the facilities. But you'll need to bear in mind where your water will come from (think about how you'll cope if there's a hosepipe ban) and how you'll haul in compost.

RULES AND REGULATIONS

You will not face many restrictions in your own garden, but a front garden that looks like an unkempt allotment may draw unwanted attention from your neighbours. If you are renting your house, you'll have to discuss your plans with your landlord. For balconies, fire escapes and roof gardens you need to make sure that the structure can take the weight of pots of wet soil.

Pocket Fact

There are no specific laws against having a bonfire in your own garden, or when you can have one – but there are acts that deal with the risk smoke can cause to traffic, and the environmental impact of poisonous fumes.

WHAT IS GROWN AND WHAT GROWS BEST

In gardens you can grow whichever perennial plants you desire, as they're in a safe place where you can keep an eye on them. However, the built-up nature of most areas means that shade is common, and you may find that garden features cause frost pockets or wind tunnels, so you have to fine tune your planting to make the most of your microclimates.

Pocket Tip 🛒

There are many vegetables and fruits that look pretty, and make a nice addition to an ornamental garden. Think frilly lettuce, rainbow chard and striking herbs, such as bronze fennel, and edible flowers, such as calendula and nasturtiums.

Wherever you have plants in containers you have limited volumes of soil and water, so roof gardens and balconies (for example) have limits on what you can grow. Salad crops and strawberries make good use of space, and larger pots are fine for fruit bushes and larger vegetable plants – if you're prepared to keep on top of the watering and feeding.

Pocket Tip 🛒

You can buy (or construct) containers with water reservoirs at the bottom, which make watering less of a chore.

♛ SHARED ♛

WHERE THEY'RE FOUND

Where allotment demand outstrips supply and waiting lists are very long, or in inner cities where the number of allotments is limited, there are a number of local organisations that share land with people who want to grow their own food. These schemes provide access to community gardens or shared allotment plots.

Shared schemes

The Landshare scheme is a nationwide scheme which aims to put people who want to garden in touch with people who have land to share, whether it's an underused allotment site or an overgrown garden. The format is similar to online classified ads, but with plenty of support available. Visit www.landshare.net for more information.

Pocket Tip 🛒

The Landshare scheme even has its own iPhone app, so you can keep an eye on what's available, wherever you are.

Community Supported Agriculture schemes

Community Supported Agriculture schemes allow customers to support their local farmers, by buying a share of the harvest upfront, signing up for a regular box delivery scheme, or even lending a hand with the growing. The Soil Association (www.soilassociation.org) is a good place to start looking for further information.

Some city farms offer gardening opportunities to volunteers. Get in touch with a local city farm to see what they offer.

Guerrilla gardeners

You could also choose to become a guerrilla gardener – gardening on land which you do not own or have legal access to. Gardening in public spaces (unused council flower beds and planters, for example, or the tree pits that line your street) is unlikely to get you into too much trouble if you're enhancing the local area. Unauthorised access to private property is a more serious undertaking though. For more information, see the Guerrilla Gardening website (www.guerillagardening.org).

Pocket Fact 🪏

In some places dedicated guerrilla gardeners have become locally recognised, and have been allowed to continue cultivating their plots with the blessing of the owner or the local authorities.

TYPICAL LAYOUT AND FEATURES

Community gardens are intended primarily to be a green space for local residents, and often have lots of ornamental features as well as vegetable plots. They're a space for self-expression, as well, with many local artists turning their hands to decorating sheds or making bespoke fencing. Often right in the heart of communities, but hidden away unless you know they're there, they are also hubs for local gatherings, with lots of events and open days on offer.

Community schemes often have a specific focus, depending on local needs. They may offer gardening therapy to those in need, or produce enough fruits and vegetables to run a box delivery scheme for much of the year. There is likely to be an emphasis on the environment, with organic gardening and recycling the order of the day.

RULES AND REGULATIONS

Community groups have to abide by health and safety regulations, so there may be a long list of rules to remember. What you can do in a community garden will also be far more controlled than on an allotment, as you're gardening in a shared space rather than doing your own thing.

Each scheme will have its own rules and guidelines, which will be given to you when you sign up. You may have to agree to contribute a certain number of working hours in return for your share.

Pocket Tip 🛒

The Landshare scheme is merely a tool to discover available land in your local area — you need to remember that you'll be entering into an agreement with a private citizen if you use their garden, so make sure you know what's acceptable and what isn't before you start.

Guerrilla gardening is usually done as a political statement, protesting the lack of public access to the land. On publicly owned land you may simply be considered a nuisance by the local council if you garden in flower beds or containers that they should be looking after. If you trespass onto private property for your garden, you risk arrest.

WHAT IS GROWN AND WHAT GROWS BEST

Shared gardens are very variable, and what you can grow and what grows best will be different from place to place. Perennial planting may be encouraged in community gardens, or you may be limited to choosing short-term plants if you're given a specific plot.

As part of a shared scheme you may have input into what is grown, but once the plan is put in place you will simply be a willing worker. If you find your plot via Landshare, it's likely to be a cross between an allotment (which discourages you from growing expensive long-term plants) and a garden (which you'll have to keep tidy).

Guerrilla gardeners always live with the risk that their garden will be vandalised or removed (or even replanted by the rightful owner), and should plant accordingly. Their choice of plants is also limited by the lack of facilities – shallow soil and having to carry your own water makes drought-tolerant plants a must.

♛ DECIDING WHICH TYPE ♛ IS RIGHT FOR YOU

LOCATION

The best choice for an allotment or vegetable garden location is one that you can access regularly. It's important to consider how you'll get to your plot – particularly if you have tools or sundries to take with you, or heavy harvests to bring home.

There may be an allotment site just round the corner, or on your way to and from work or college. If you have to go out of your way to get to your patch then you'll need far more willpower to visit regularly.

Visit your local sites to find out which one is best for you. Do you feel safe in that area, even when it's dark? Is there too much traffic on that road for you to cycle there comfortably? If you want to drive to the site, is there an area where you can park the car?

TIME

One of the key things a kitchen garden of any size needs is regular attention. It can survive alone for a couple of weeks when you're on holiday (with the right preparation), but any garden that is neglected becomes over-run with weeds and pests. On an allotment site this may even lead to you losing your plot, so be realistic about the amount of time you can spend there, and hence the amount of land you can cultivate.

Taking on a whole allotment plot, particularly one that is already overgrown, is a considerable undertaking and often enough to put newcomers off as they struggle (usually over the winter, in the worst of the weather) to get the soil ready for planting.

The National Society of Allotment and Leisure Gardeners (NSALG) recommends you spend a minimum of two hours a week on an allotment, but the more time you can spend there the better your plot will be. Bear in mind that the busiest periods of the year for kitchen gardeners are spring and summer.

Pocket Tip 🛒

If you're unsure about making such a large time commitment then look for a smaller plot to begin with, and upgrade if you really get the bug.

MONEY

The best approach to covering the costs of your new allotment is to decide on a yearly budget. It's easy to overdo things (especially at the beginning) and buy too many tools, plants, seeds and sundries which means that you spend more money on the plot than the resulting produce is worth.

On an allotment site you have to pay the rent in advance, but you may then be able to borrow, swap and barter to cover most of your needs. The allotment mentality of recycling means that DIY structures are usually perfectly acceptable as long as your plot looks well tended.

Using your own garden or space avoids the rent, and allows you to spend money on prized plants that you may not feel comfortable growing on an allotment. But you almost certainly won't have the space to make tons of compost, and will need to budget for potting compost or top soil. Containers can be very expensive, particularly large ones, although it is possible to recycle food containers to do the job.

If you have a water meter, you'll need to factor in the expense of watering your plants in dry weather. If you're using public transport to travel to your plot, you'll need to budget for that, too.

LEVEL OF EXPERTISE

It is easy to be bewildered by the depth of knowledge on display from gardening old-hands or even 'basic' gardening manuals, but the truth of the matter is that enthusiasm and effort count for far more on an allotment than years of experience. It's important not to try to do too much too soon, and become discouraged, but there's nothing about growing your own vegetables that is too hard for a beginner to tackle.

All you need to bring a large plot into productive cultivation is the time and energy to dig it over, remove the weeds and add compost or manure as necessary to improve the soil fertility.

That being said, one of the important skills to learn is getting the timing right, knowing when to sow, plant and harvest, and you may find this easier if you only grow one or two crops to begin with. Buying plants to transplant is a little bit more expensive, but might get you off to a flying start if you're finding the idea of sowing all those seeds rather daunting.

Annual plants are very forgiving – a mistake this year just means you'll be more experienced next season. Perennial plants are often less work in the long run, but only if they're happy where they're planted – so you may want to leave those until you feel a bit more confident. Fruit trees and bushes will need pruning in future years, which is another skill that looks tricky but is easily learned.

While you're searching for your perfect plot, why not borrow a gardening book from the library, or sow a few seeds on the windowsill, so you have a grasp of the basics?

Pocket Tip 🛞

Many people find that gardening reduces stress. To get the most out of it, make sure that your plot is a fun and enjoyable place to be, not an endless list of chores.

3

HOW TO FIND AND PICK AN ALLOTMENT

In theory there should be an allotment for everyone who wants one. In practice, there are many places with long waiting lists, and many plots that are simply too much to take on (because they're waterlogged, desperately weedy or covered in junk). Although the long waiting lists may tempt you to go for the first plot you're offered, you need to make sure it's the right one for you. In this chapter we look at how to find the right plot for you.

♛ WAITING LISTS ♛

LOCAL AUTHORITIES

Your first port of call to find an allotment may be your local authority, particularly if you're looking for an urban site. Allotments are rented out by parish, town, borough, city or district councils. If you're not sure where to start, have a look at the DirectGov website (www.direct.gov.uk/en/Dl1/Directories/Localcouncils/index.htm), which has lists of the main local councils and their contact details. Most will have information about allotments, and a point of contact, listed on their website. Otherwise a quick phone call will elicit all of the information you need.

You may find that all of the local allotments are administered by the council, or that they are run by their allotment society. In this case you will need to contact the allotment secretary to find out whether plots are available and to be put on the waiting list if not.

If you know where allotment sites are, you can also drop in. If they're actively recruiting new plotholders, the contact details will be displayed on a sign or notice board, but you can also speak to existing allotmenteers to find out about any availabilities.

Pocket Tip 🛒

Waiting lists full of people who have lost interest, or who have moved, are the bane of an allotment secretary's life. Keep in regular contact to prove you're keen and you may jump to the top of the list.

A useful organisation if you're plot hunting is NSALG, the National Society of Allotment and Leisure Gardeners. Its website (www.nsalg.org.uk) is packed with useful information to help you find a plot and get growing. If you're in Scotland, you'll need to contact SAGS, the Scottish Allotments and Gardens Society (www.sags.org.uk).

COUNTRYSIDE

If an allotment site is already set up on farmland then you'll need to speak to the farmer about getting a plot – ask one of the existing plotholders for the contact information.

If there's an unused field on your local farm, you may like to talk to the farmer about setting up new allotments. You may have to visit the farm in person or do some detective work to track down the details.

For other privately owned sites, eg British Waterways or Network Rail, you'll have to contact the landowner directly.

Pocket Tip 🛒

Your local gardening association is a good place to ask for help if you're having trouble finding a plot. Sometimes it's a case of who you know!

SHARED

If you're interested in sharing a private garden, you may already know a neighbour with more space than they can care for. Otherwise there are two websites you can use to find a local garden share, or register your interest.

- Landshare (www.landshare.net) – this is the most well-known scheme, having been publicised by Hugh Fearnley-Whittingstall from River Cottage.

- I Dig Allotments (www.idigallotments.co.uk/index.php) – this is another useful site.

There may be more local schemes that can help. Have a look at the notice board at the local library or community centre and see whether you're covered by a Transition Towns group (it focuses on sustainable living, including local food projects).

The Federation of City Farms and Community Gardens (http://farmgarden.org.uk) can also help you find shared gardens across the UK, and its website includes a search facility. The federation also hosts the Allotments Regeneration Initiative (http://farmgarden.org.uk/ari), which is useful if you're thinking of creating or regenerating an allotment site.

Pocket Tip 🖐

If you're based in London, try Capital Growth (www.capitalgrowth.org), which aims to support 2,012 new community food gardens by the end of 2012.

Local environmental groups (including the local branches of nationwide groups) may also be able to help you find a community garden or shared scheme.

♕ THE FINE PRINT ♕

Once you've found an available plot, you should review the terms of your rental agreement and consider all of the legal aspects associated with taking on the plot.

CHECKING YOUR RIGHTS AND RENTAL AGREEMENT

Your allotment rental agreement might be quite short, or very involved, depending on the site. It should lay out your responsibilities – which are likely to include ensuring that your plot is kept tidy and under cultivation, and that you adhere to the security arrangements (keeping gates locked etc). It should also outline what you are and aren't allowed to grow, and if you can keep animals.

Pocket Fact ⬖

If you don't keep up with your responsibilities, you could lose your plot. You should be given a warning but you may simply get a month's notice, depending on the nature of your infringement.

Your agreement should also tell you how to terminate it. On a local authority allotment you should get a year's notice of losing your plot if there has been no breach of the agreement (eg if the land is being sold).

KNOWING YOUR RIGHTS

All councils (except inner London) have a legal obligation to provide allotments if there is a demand. If your council does not offer allotments, or there are long waiting lists, then any group of adults who are registered for council tax can request that allotments are provided.

Pocket Tip ⬖

Requesting a new allotment site is a formal procedure – check the NSALG website for more details on how to go about it, or ask SAGS if you're in Scotland.

You do not have the right to sub-let your plot, or pass your tenancy on to a specific person – if you release your plot it normally goes to the next person on the waiting list. You may also be prevented from using your plot as a commercial market garden.

The laws governing allotments are complicated, so if you have a problem that cannot be resolved with your allotment association then contact NSALG or SAGS for further advice.

♛ AVERAGE COSTS ♛

Allotment rents are usually a fraction of the value of the produce you can hope to grow each year, but you should always consider the costs of having an allotment before you agree to take one on. For those allotments owned and run by local authorities, rents are typically £20–£50 per year, paid in advance. Privately owned allotments could cost as much as £150 a year though.

On top of your rent you may have to pay a deposit for a gate key (or a key to access the water supply), and be asked for a small contribution to the allotment committee, which is used towards communal extras.

You'll need a basic set of tools to start work – a spade and fork for digging, and a trowel for planting. You may also need a rake, wheelbarrow and watering can or hosepipe. Other tools can be bought or borrowed as and when they're needed, and it's easy to bring produce home in carrier bags or cardboard boxes. A compost bin is not necessary (a heap will do fine), and both they and water butts are often offered on Freegle (www.ilovefreegle.org) or Freecycle (www.uk.freecycle.org) if you can collect them.

Typical equipment costs

- *Spade or fork: £8–£25*
- *Trowel: £5–£10*
- *Rake: £10–£2*
- *Wheelbarrow: £25–£50*
- *Watering can: £5–£15*

Pocket Tip 🖐

A lot of gardening tools are available second-hand, but be wary of places such as car boot sales as they provide an easy way for thieves to sell off tools they have stolen from local allotment sites.

Seeds are usually £1–£3 per packet, depending on what you buy and from where. For most plots, a packet of seed will be more than enough for a year, so you can either share with friends or save seeds for the following year. Seed potatoes and onion sets are a little bit more expensive, but still only a few pounds. Fruit trees and bushes do cost more (a lot more work has gone into producing them), but you can shop around for good deals and they remain productive for years.

Pocket Tip 🖐

Tools, sheds and even plants may be covered by your household insurance if they're in your garden, but you may want to investigate additional insurance before you take them to your allotment.

♛ HOW TO PICK THE BEST ♛ ALLOTMENT FOR YOU

Even though allotments are in short supply in many places, there is no requirement for you to take the first plot that you're offered. It may be too overgrown for a newcomer to take on, or strewn with rubbish you may never be able to clear. If it's overhung by trees then it may be too shady, with the tree roots sucking all of the goodness out of the soil. A plot in the corner may make you feel insecure, and a frost pocket or badly drained area adds to the challenge.

Have a chat with your prospective neighbours, and they can give you the low-down on the offered plot. Take their advice into consideration along with all of the other factors (location, time, money, expertise) and make an informed choice.

Pocket Tip

It is better to wait for the right plot to come along, than struggle with the wrong plot and become discouraged.

4

PLANNING AND MANAGING YOUR ALLOTMENT

Once you've found your plot it's time to take stock and think about how to make the most of your space. In this chapter you'll find information about assessing and clearing your site, planning what to grow and keeping your soil healthy.

♕ ASSESSING YOUR SITE ♕

You may inherit an allotment that has been well cared for. However, it's more usual to be given a neglected, weedy patch that is gearing up to be declared a Site of Special Scientific Interest. It's tempting to hire a rotavator (mechanical digger) or reach for the weedkiller, but take a few moments to survey the site first.

Walk the boundaries of the plot so that you know what is yours (if they're not clearly marked then ask for clarification). Do a quick sketch and mark in plants that can't be moved eg fruit bushes, asparagus and rhubarb. Add in the compost bins, and the shed if you're lucky enough to have one.

Look at the soil. If you dig a small hole, does it look dark and fertile, or pale and unhealthy? See the next section on soil for help in figuring out which type you have on your allotment.

Pocket Tip 🖐
Don't rush into sowing or planting — time spent planning now pays dividends later.

Check your access to facilities: does your site have toilets, a shop, tools to borrow or hire? You should also find your nearest water supply.

Have a chat with your neighbours, who can tell you what grows well, which diseases are rife and the recent history of your patch. There may also be free deliveries of manure, compost and bark chips, so ask about those.

SOIL

It's possible that the previous tenant of your plot grew nothing but potatoes, or treated their soil to a flood of chemicals that have left it too barren to grow much at all without more of the same. An allotment full of weeds at least indicates that the soil is fertile enough to support plants! Before you can begin planting you need to figure out what type of soil you have and plan your crops accordingly.

Sandy soil

Dig a small hole and have a look at the soil. Is it dry, even underneath the surface? Is it crumbly and gritty? If so you have a sandy soil, which drains well and is never waterlogged. Sandy soil warms up quickly in spring and is great for getting off to a good start, but it doesn't hold water and plants may be thirsty in hot weather.

Clay soil

If it's summer and your soil is baked hard with huge cracks running through it, then you have clay soil. In winter it will be cold and wet under the surface. If you pick up a small handful of soil, the easier it is to work your sample into a ball, the more clay it contains. Clay soil takes longer to warm up in spring, but holds water better in summer (until it dries out, then it takes a lot of water to turn it back into soil again). The advantage of clay soil is that it contains more plant nutrients.

Acidity

If your plot has been in use for a few years then you'll know that it can successfully be used to grow vegetables, which means that its pH value (how acid or alkaline it is) is within a certain range. The quickest way to find out whether it's acid or alkaline is to ask a gardening neighbour, but you can also get a test kit (like a mini chemistry set) or probe to check it out for yourself. It's not urgent that you do so, but it tells you whether you can grow crops such as blueberries, which are choosy about their soil requirements. Most common vegetables aren't that fussy, although many do better under certain conditions.

Pocket Fact

The pH scale runs from 0 to 14, and the lower numbers are more acidic. Most common vegetables prefer soil that is nearly neutral: close to 7 on the pH scale.

Whether your soil is sandy and dry, heavy and full of clay or a certain pH value, you're stuck with it. Changing it on a large scale is a big job, and unnecessary. But all soils benefit from having organic matter (eg compost) added. Organic matter helps sandy soils retain moisture and nutrients, makes clay soils drain better, and encourages the ecosystem of organisms that live in healthy soil and support plant growth. It's magic stuff!

ASPECT

Like soil, one thing you can't really change is your aspect. Whether you have acres of space, or a tiny courtyard, the aspect (whether it's north- or south-facing) is set. You have to work with what you have.

North-facing plots

A north-facing aspect gives you a cool garden that may be prone to frost and shade. Too much shade will limit the types of crops you can grow, but leafy vegetables such as lettuce and oriental salad leaves love the cool. Herbs such as mint and lemon balm will also thrive.

South-facing plots

Many plants prefer a south-facing aspect, which is sunnier (particularly in the winter) and warmer. Tender annuals such as tomatoes and peppers will enjoy basking in the sun, and a south-facing sheltered spot may be ideal for more unusual crops such as melons and sweet potatoes. However, sunny patches dry out much more quickly in hot weather, and require more watering.

Microclimates

You may have damp patches, or dry areas, and slopes and contours that channel water. Buildings and trees cast shade. All of these affect what you can grow, but unless your entire patch is in deep shade all summer, you're not going to have much trouble finding plants that can thrive in your conditions.

Pocket Tip

A dip or slope can channel and hold frost — a 'frost pocket' is a cold patch in your garden, so you wouldn't plant a peach tree there, but it's fine for hardy vegetables.

Now that you've made an initial assessment of your plot, including its soil and aspect, you can begin to clear it and start planning your delicious produce.

♕ WEEDS ♕

Unless your plot was cultivated recently, one of your first tasks will be to deal with the weeds. First you have to know your enemy; borrow a guide to weeds from the library and identify the ones growing on your plot.

Weeds can be divided into several categories but the most useful distinction is between annual and perennial weeds.

ANNUAL WEEDS

Annual weeds live their entire life in one year. They're easy to hoe off, bury or pull up, but their seeds survive in soil for years, just waiting for the soil to be turned over so they can see the light.

Annual weeds colonise bare soil, so keeping it covered reduces your weed problems. However, you can't grow seeds in soil that has been covered over. This technique is called a 'Stale Seedbed': uncovering the soil, giving the weed seeds time to germinate and then hoeing them off. You then sow your seeds, knowing that most of the weeds are already gone.

Pocket Fact ❧

Biennial weeds complete their lifecycle over two years.

PERENNIAL WEEDS

Perennial weeds have a long-term strategy. These are the weeds that people curse about. Dandelions have long tap roots that snap if you pull them, and then regrow. Couch grass roots survive being chopped up. Brambles bend over and root where they touch the soil. Bindweed smothers everything in sight. If you're digging, you need to pull out every section of root you can see, then wait for the ones you missed to regrow. Even if you reach for the weed-killer in desperation, a fight against perennial weeds requires patience.

Pocket Fact ❧

Brambles can grow 8cm (3 inches) a day – you can almost see them growing!

DISPOSAL

Annual weeds that aren't setting seed can go on the compost heap. Send perennial weeds and seeding weeds off for commercial composting or drown them in a bucket of water for several weeks. If you're feeling battered by the weed war then have a bonfire (if you're allowed) and burn the blighters. You can also incarcerate them in a black plastic sack and leave it behind the shed. In a couple of years' time they will have become compost.

CLEARING THE SPACE

In areas with annual weeds you can safely dig over the soil, whether by hand or mechanically. If you have perennial weeds, mechanical digging chops up their roots and spreads them far and wide; careful manual digging and removal of the roots is a better option.

Pocket Fact

A single couch grass plant can have 154m (505 feet) of rhizomes (underground stems).

That may sound like a lot of work, and it is, but you don't need to do it all at once. You can kill most weeds with almost no work and a little patience, if you cover them over and exclude light. You can buy black plastic sheeting to do the job, or get the same effect entirely free if you collect cardboard or newspaper. Cover an area thoroughly (weeds are notorious for finding any chinks) with the cardboard and then cover that with a thick layer of compost or grass cuttings. This covering layer is called a mulch, and gradually breaks down into the soil. Clearing your plot this way is an example of 'no dig gardening' (see p.41 for more on this).

Pocket Tip

You can plant potatoes, and strong plants such as pumpkins, through your mulch.

By covering sections of the plot you eliminate most weeding and can concentrate on clearing sections as you need them.

♛ PLANNING YOUR CROPS ♛

Traditionally an allotment is managed according to a set routine, year after year, providing staple vegetables for a family. That option gives you a very easy-to-follow plan, but tastes change over the years and you may not find it appealing. There's no reason why you can't produce something more exotic from your plot.

Planning starts with some easy steps:

● Write down what your family likes to eat. Think seasonally: most people want salads in the summer and hearty root vegetables in the winter, but there are salad crops that grow year round, and plenty of stir-fry vegetables, too.

● When you go shopping make a note of what you buy. It's also helpful to know which fruits and vegetables are the most expensive. Often they are too exotic to grow well here, but some don't transport well, or are hard to harvest mechanically, and if you grow those you can save yourself some money.

● You also need to think about how many plants of each type of vegetable you want. You'll probably want a regular supply of lettuces, but if you plant more than a couple of courgettes then friends will run away when they see you – courgette gluts are widespread in summer.

Pocket Tip 🛞

Don't get bogged down in the details – the joy of gardening is that mistakes can be rectified next year, if not sooner.

BEING REALISTIC

It's easy to get carried away when you're planning, but be realistic about the time you have available; think about how much time you'll have in a good week, and in a bad week. Pick plants that would be happy with that, and grow them in the right place.

It's important, in the beginning, not to overestimate what you can do and be realistic about your skill level. Start small and increase your space as you get the hang of things. Also, just because your neighbour, friend or favourite television gardener says a plant is easy to grow, it doesn't mean it will thrive in your garden, and failing to grow it well doesn't make you a bad gardener.

Skill level	Plot size	Crops
Beginners	A bed 1m–2m in size is easy to manage and can be very productive.	Salad leaves, tomatoes, strawberries, French beans and herbs in containers.
Improvers	Add a second bed, or take on half an allotment. Rotate your crops.	Root crops, potatoes, onions, garlic, rhubarb, raspberries.
Advanced	A large garden or full-sized allotment. Grow a wide variety of crops.	Asparagus, artichokes, cabbages, cauliflower.

VEGETABLE FAMILIES

Every fruit, vegetable and herb belongs to a family of related plants. Some bear an obvious resemblance to their relatives; others are more of a surprise.

Vegetables in the same plant family often have the same requirements, so it can be helpful to be aware of the families and grow them together. However, the same families may also be prone to the same pests and diseases, which build up over time, so vegetable families are moved around the plot each year, in a rotation (see p.41 for more).

Common vegetable families

The potato family
Potatoes, tomatoes, peppers (sweet and chilli), aubergines

The cabbage family
Cabbages, kale, broccoli, Brussels sprouts, many oriental vegetables, radishes, turnips, kohl rabi

The marrow family
Courgettes, marrows, squashes and pumpkins, cucumbers, melons

Peas and beans
Peas, broad beans, French beans, runner beans

The onion family
Onions, spring onions, leeks, garlic, shallots, chives

The beet family
Beetroot, spinach, chard, leaf beet

The carrot family
Carrots, parsnips, celery and many herbs, including parsley, chervil, coriander, fennel

The lettuce family
Lettuce and endive, artichokes, chicory, plus many flowers, including marigolds, sunflowers, dahlias

Pocket Tip

It takes a very serious scientist (a taxonomist) to put the right plant in the right plant family; and even they keep changing their minds! You don't need to remember them all, just be aware of the general grouping.

PLANNING BY LOCATION

Patios and gardens

A back garden, or patio, has one advantage over an allotment: it may be small, but it's right outside your back door. You can water pots most days, and harvest quick-growing crops such as salad leaves at their best. Gardening can be done in short bursts, and this is an ideal place for plants that 'bolt' to the finish line, as you can stop them in their tracks.

Plot

If your plot is a distance away then you won't be there as often, although you're likely to be there for longer. As it won't benefit from constant attention, it's a great place to grow crops that thrive largely on their own. Weeding and harvesting once or twice a week is fine if you grow plants that have a slightly slower pace of life.

Pocket Tip

Potatoes, pumpkins and perennials such as rhubarb and soft fruit are just some of the plants that don't need constant attention.

♛ DESIGNING A LAYOUT ♛

A traditional vegetable garden has long, straight rows of each vegetable (an 'open layout'). The advantage of this method is that it's easy to spot when some of the plants aren't doing as well as they should. The problem with this method is that it's easy for everyone else to spot when some of the plants aren't doing as well as they should! It also encourages weeds, and you'll spend a lot of time hoeing the weeds and trampling the soil.

An open layout is fine for an allotment, but in a garden you may prefer to keep things neater. A raised bed is a marked-out bed that, by the regular addition of compost, becomes higher than the surrounding paths. You can edge your beds (on allotments, scaffolding boards are popular), but that can be expensive and isn't necessary. Each bed should be no wider than a metre or so, so that you can reach into the middle without stepping on the soil. All work is done from the path. Use paths to divide the plot into at least four sections, so that you can rotate crops around the plot (explained in more detail later in the chapter).

Pocket Tip 🛒

If you inherit a layout with wider beds, add stepping stones to work from.

Allocate each of your plant families a bed or section of the plot, and you have your site plan for the year. If you enjoy planning then you can work out which vegetables have to be planted when, which gives you a sowing timetable and maps out the whole year in advance.

If you feel overwhelmed by all the planning, or are a free spirit, then you can wing it – most seeds need to be sown during spring and you can copy what everyone else is doing or work out the right time for planting spuds (for example) by seeing what's on offer at the garden centre.

HERBS

For herbs, the most important distinction is whether they are perennial, and need a permanent home, or whether they are annual (or biennial) plants that are replaced each year and can be moved around.

Herbs also differ widely in their requirements. The so-called Mediterranean herbs like a sunny spot and well-drained soil. These include rosemary, thyme and lavender. If you buy one of these plants, it usually says 'Full Sun' on the label.

Many herbs from closer to home cope with 'Partial Shade' (a less sunny spot) and require more water. Parsley, chervil and all of the mints slurp down far more water than their counterparts from sunnier climes.

Pocket Tip 🛒

There has to be an exception, and it's basil. It loves heat and sunshine, but needs plenty of water to thrive!

Given the right amount of sun and water all of these herbs can grow in pots in smaller gardens. The advantage of this is that you can bring the tender ones inside for the winter, ensuring their survival and continuing supplies for the kitchen. The disadvantage is that you'll need to replace even perennial plants every few years, as they outgrow your space.

FRUIT

Fruit plants are divided into soft fruit and tree fruit. Soft fruit either grows on small plants (eg strawberries) or in bushes (eg raspberries, gooseberries and the currants). Popular tree fruit include apples, pears, cherries and plums, but you should check your lease to find out whether trees are welcome on your plot.

Strawberries can be grown anywhere, as they are low-growing and happy in pots. They like a sunny spot. Other soft fruits are happiest with their roots in open soil, although you can grow blueberries and cranberries in containers.

You can now get almost any kind of fruit tree in any size: from tiny trees for patio pots through to trees that top out at head height and bear all their fruit within easy reach. Many fruit trees can be trained over a wall or fence so that they take up very little space, but they do have to be kept pruned.

When planning your fruit garden, bear in mind that many fruit plants need a pollination partner, unless the variety you choose is marked as 'self-fertile' (see box below for more on this). Even so, many self-fertile plants are more productive when planted with a suitable partner.

Pollination

Flowers are a plant's method of reproduction. For a flower to produce seed it needs to be pollinated, where pollen from the male parts of the flower (or a male flower) is transferred to the female parts (or female flower). This job is often done by insects such as bees. Plants that are self-fertile can pollinate themselves; for other plants you will need a pair to ensure cross-pollination.

♛ DIGGING ♛

To dig, or not to dig: that is the question. Traditionally, vegetable gardens were dug over every year. Digging allows weeds to be removed, manure to be incorporated and the freshly dug soil to settle to a 'fine tilth' (texture) over winter, which is perfect for sowing seeds in spring. You can even 'double dig', which involves turning over the heavy subsoil rather than just the nice topsoil that plants sink their roots into. Digging is hard work, but good exercise (if you do it properly) and a well-dug plot can provide a giant sense of achievement.

There is another school of thought though. Soil isn't simply something we poke plants into, it's a living ecosystem in its own right. It supports micro-organisms, fungi and creepy-crawlies, all of whom contribute to keeping the soil healthy. Disturbing this web of life leaves a soil that is less capable of supporting healthy plants. People who believe this dig their soil as little as possible, often never.

If your allotment is weedy then you may want to dig to make space for your plants. You can try the 'no dig' alternative, covering the ground with a thick mulch, that excludes light and prevents weeds from growing (as discussed on p.34). It's slower, but easier and less time-consuming in the long run. Once your plot is weed-free, it's easy enough to keep it that way without digging, so you may want to leave the spade in the shed and let nature dig your soil for you.

♛ CROP ROTATION ♛

Crop rotation is a way of taking into account the different nutritional needs of different vegetables, by planting them in rotation on a particular patch of soil. It also allows you to add things such as manure and lime at the right time for the plants that need them. Some plants are more adept at shading out weeds than others, so rotating them around also helps you keep on top of that issue.

BASIC FOUR-YEAR ROTATION

A basic four-year rotation for a cool climate such as Britain's involves four different beds or areas. The plan for the first year looks like this:

Bed 1	Bed 2
Potato and marrow families	Carrot and beet families
Bed 4	**Bed 3**
Onion family, peas and beans	Cabbage family

Bed 1 is manured in spring, before you plant the potatoes. Bed 4 has garden lime added in autumn (if necessary, to raise the pH) after the crops have been harvested. Then everything moves one place clockwise each year.

However, if you slavishly follow a suggested rotation then you're bound to run into problems. Perhaps your areas aren't all the same size, or you don't have four beds. Perhaps you don't have space for potatoes, or you don't eat cabbages. Design your own rotation, taking into account what you want to grow and which plants do well together. Then simply move them to a different patch next year.

Pocket Tip 🛒

You may have noticed that the lettuce family isn't on the rotation. Lettuces are fitted in anywhere there's space!

If you're growing in containers then you don't have to worry about rotations. Simply recycle your potting mix via the compost heap and make sure that any perennial plants get a top-dressing of fresh compost, and some fertiliser, in spring.

♛ COMPOST ♛

You don't need a compost bin to make compost, you can simply make a compost heap. A compost bin keeps things neater and makes compost more quickly, but the method you use is a matter of choice. Plastic compost bins are cheap and make good use of space. In a garden you may want something more attractive.

Ideally a compost bin stands on soil in a sunny spot. In practice you can make compost wherever you have space, even on concrete, but it does take longer for the compost to form in the shade.

HOT COMPOSTING

Making a hot compost heap that devours anything organic in a matter of days is a labour of love. You construct the heap carefully, with the right materials in even layers. You wait for it to heat up, then start to cool down, and then you have to turn it to mix up the layers. And then you do it again. Finally you relax and let it mature for several weeks before use.

COLD COMPOSTING

Most people don't have the time, the energy, or the right mix of materials for hot composting and so take the more relaxed option of cold composting. With cold composting you throw materials in as and when you have them, and let it decompose in its own time. The average household naturally produces a good mixture of materials (see p.44).

Different materials take differing amounts of time to break down, and you may find that when you come to use your compost that it's still a bit lumpy. You can screen out the big bits (if you want to) and throw them back in to break down further. Everything organic rots, eventually.

THINGS TO COMPOST

Compost breaks down because bacteria, fungi and mini-beasts eat organic matter. They need a balanced diet of browns and greens (about equal amounts, by volume).

Browns (carbon-rich materials)	**Greens** (full of nitrogen)
Twigs	Fresh leaves and stems
Dead leaves	Grass cuttings
Cardboard	Vegetable peelings
Newspaper	Apple cores
Straw	Tea leaves
Hay	Coffee grounds
Wood shavings	Faeces from vegetarian animals

You can also add egg shells, which add calcium, but crush them up as they're slow to break down.

Pocket Tip

Don't compost cat and dog faeces, meat, fish or dairy products – they smell nasty as they rot and attract vermin.

WORM COMPOSTING

If you have a small garden then a worm composter may be for you. Composting worms eat their way through kitchen waste (and a small amount of garden waste) to produce small volumes of compost and a liquid plant feed. They don't take up much space, but as they're living creatures you need to ensure they have food, air and water and that they don't bake or freeze.

♛ BONFIRES ♛

You can reuse or recycle a lot of the 'rubbish' found or produced on your plot. Be creative and use it to build useful structures – it's 'allotment chic'. There may also be occasional rubbish collections.

Composting, shredding and mulching deals with all of the plant waste. Sometimes though you'll need to get rid of waste and your best option may be a bonfire.

Many allotment sites do not allow bonfires, but if yours does and you want to dispose of waste this way then follow these safety tips.

- Check piles of waste for wildlife (particularly hibernating hedgehogs in winter) before lighting.

- Keep a bucket of water on hand.

- Keep smoke to a minimum (only burn dry waste).

- Don't leave fires unattended. Make sure they're truly out.

- Don't use liquid fuels such as petrol or paraffin as accelerants. If you're struggling, use firelighters.

- Keep your fire level and away from overhanging branches.

- Don't burn rubbish that may be toxic, extremely flammable or dangerous (no aerosols or plastics).

- Don't start fires on windy days.

Consider buying a garden incinerator, or making one out of an old metal dustbin or barrel, to keep fires contained. You can add the ashes to the compost heap once they're cold.

Pocket Tip 🖐

Collect falling leaves in autumn and compost them separately to form leaf mould, which makes a great mulch or soil improver.

5

ESSENTIAL TOOLS AND EQUIPMENT

It's easy to spend a lot of money on tools and equipment for your allotment, some of which you'll never need and many of which simply aren't worth the money. In this chapter we look at the essential tools you'll need to manage your plot, plus the ones that are 'nice to have'.

♛ ESSENTIAL TOOLS ♛

Garden centres and catalogues sell a bewildering supply of tools and sundries. Some are essential and will become firm favourites. Others have a limited use or lifespan, but there are plenty that you can make yourself (see p.57 for ideas).

Top ten 'must have' tools

1. **Trowel**. *Essential for planting out and endlessly useful elsewhere.*
2. **Secateurs**. *Used for chopping back tough weeds, harvesting crops and generally tidying up.*
3. **Spade**. *Unless you have a very small space, a spade is a must for digging and planting.*
4. **Fork**. *A garden fork makes digging easier on heavy soil. A hand fork is useful for weeding or on small plots.*
5. **Watering can**. *You can use a bucket and a dipper, but a watering can directs water exactly where you want it.*
6. **Hoe**. *A good hoe makes light work of weeding; essential on large plots.*

---

7. **Rake**. Useful for preparing beds for planting and sowing, as well as clearing up.
8. **String**. For tying plants into supports, use a biodegradable twine, as it's likely to end up on the compost heap at some point.
9. **Canes**. Used for supporting individual plants or building supporting structures.
10. **Gloves**. Although there's nothing wrong with getting your hands dirty, some tasks (eg turning compost and removing brambles) demand some protection.

Pocket Tip 🛒

When you're putting your tools away for the winter, make sure they're clean – they'll last much longer. Clean off the dirt, oil wooden handles and store metal tools in a bucket of sand that you've added a couple of glugs of oil to. They'll be clean and ready to use come spring.

Top ten 'nice to have' tools

1. **Wheelbarrow**. Endlessly useful for carting things about, especially if your plot is a trek from the gate. They do vary, so try a few to get one that suits you as some are easier to steer and tip than others.
2. **Pocket knife**. A proper folding pocket knife makes you feel like a proper gardener and makes short work of cutting through string or soft plant material.
3. **Riddle**. A large sieve, designed to separate lumps in homemade compost. You can get sets, with different grades, if you want to make your own potting mixes.
4. **Shears**. Make cutting back rampant growth much quicker.
5. **Dibber**. Essentially a shaped stick that is used to make sowing holes of various sizes.

6. **Trug**. *A traditional shallow basket for harvesting produce.*
7. **String dispenser**. *Keeps your string dry and tangle-free.*
8. **Seed tin**. *Keeps your seeds dry and safe from pesky rodents.*
9. **Notebook**. *Keep a track of what you've sown and where to avoid surprises!*
10. **Garden line**. *If you have a large plot and want straight lines then a garden line is indispensable.*

EXTENDING THE SEASON

While there are hardy vegetables that will take the worst that the British weather can throw at them, there are also plenty of crops that will thrive in chilly weather if they're given a little bit of protection. Winter salad crops are more tender if they're protected from the wind, and it's always nice to bring forward the first eagerly awaited crops of tomatoes and strawberries.

There are a number of ways to extend the season, all of which require some equipment. In this section we look at the pros and cons of the main types of equipment used for extending the season.

GREENHOUSES

A greenhouse (or glasshouse) is a permanent structure with a minimal frame and rigid glazing, traditionally made of glass, but increasingly made of plastic. The aim is to let in as much light as possible, whilst providing protection from the elements. A greenhouse can be staggeringly hot in summer, and without any form of heating can get very cold in winter.

A greenhouse is often a must-have in a garden, but they're rarely seen on allotments due to the investment required and the breakable nature of the glazing panes. Polytunnels are more popular on allotments.

Pocket Tip 🐄

Before investing in a greenhouse (or polytunnel) for an allotment, check your lease to make sure they're allowed.

POLYTUNNELS

A polytunnel (sometimes called a hoop house) is a bit more like a tent. It has rigid hoops over which a clear plastic sheet is stretched. Erecting anything more than the smallest models requires several pairs of hands, and should not be attempted in windy weather.

The advantage over a greenhouse is that they're cheaper, although the sheeting will need replacing after several years (and possibly patching occasionally). You do get a lot of growing room for your money, and polytunnels are popular on allotments if they are allowed.

The light inside is slightly more diffuse than in a glasshouse, which can be better for the plants as there is no need to apply shading in the summer.

HOT BEDS

Hot beds were a mainstay of the Victorian gardener, when supplies of horse manure were easy to find. The idea is to pile up fresh manure into a box (or composting bay) so as it rots down it produces heat, which can be used to start off seedlings or keep tender crops such as pineapples warm through the winter.

Once the heat starts to rise you can bury plants in pots in the top layer of manure, or pop trays of seedlings on the top. You don't want to plant directly into the manure, as it's too fresh to be good for plant roots. Add a cold frame or an old window to act as a clear lid to make the most of the heat.

You have to keep an eye on a hot bed (also known as a hot box). Once the composting is underway the temperature will start to drop and the manure needs to be turned to add enough oxygen to kick-start the process again. Come spring you'll have a supply of well-rotted manure to fertilise your beds!

Pocket Tip

For more information on how to build a hot bed, visit the Garden Organic website (www.gardenorganic.org.uk/todo_now/faqs.php?id=162).

COLD FRAMES

A cold frame is like a small greenhouse. Traditionally they are wooden frames with glass lids ('lights') that slope down from back to front. Used for raising seedlings, hardening off plants or covering winter crops, the lids are propped open to provide appropriate levels of ventilation.

A cold frame contains a small volume of air and can become a scorching death-trap for seedlings in spring, on only slightly sunny days. They can also become havens for slugs and snails, so keep an eye on them.

Pocket Fact

Cold frames are 'cold' because they are not heated. Similarly you can have 'cold' greenhouses with no heat; 'cool' greenhouses heated to keep them above freezing, and 'hot' greenhouses that are kept warm for tender plants.

Modern versions with shelves and plastic covers tend to be labelled as mini-greenhouses, but the intent is the same. You can also get ones with aluminium frames, but some are very flimsy.

CLOCHES

Victorians used large glass bell cloches to cover tender plants and keep them safe from the weather and pests. Cloches have no ventilation and can heat up very quickly; they're also expensive, breakable and heavy. The glass 'knobs' at the top can act as magnifying glasses and scorch plants. But they are very pretty and look very good in a garden setting.

A more practical cloche for an allotment is the modern plastic variety. They come in various sizes and most have vents at the top.

Plastic tunnels are merely extended cloches, and with all of them you have to ensure that enough water is reaching the plants inside.

FORCING POTS

Another familiar sight to Victorians were terracotta forcing pots, which look very similar to the bell cloches but are opaque. Their role is to force crops such as rhubarb and sea kale, which can be encouraged to grow early (and more tender) stems in the absence of light.

A forcing pot is another item that's expensive but looks great in a garden setting – the allotment version is often a large bucket or dustbin, one that's dark enough to exclude all light.

PLASTIC SHEETS, FLEECE AND MESH

Plastic sheeting can be used to warm the soil in spring, which gives you a head start on sowing your seeds. Use clear plastic for this as it allows the sun in and then traps the heat underneath. Later in the season a layer of black plastic over the soil can help crops that like long, hot summers to thrive in a mediocre British one.

Horticultural fleece is a protective fabric that allows rain and air through, but can keep frost and pests out. You can buy sheets or a roll, or specially fashioned fleece bags for individual plants.

Lighter mesh fabrics are used for insect protection in summer and also to protect seedlings and leafy salads from too much sun.

Pocket Tip 🛒

Bear in mind that garden structures (and fruit bushes) can be damaged by the weight of snow, so brush it off before it becomes too deep. You can also get plant 'cosies', or use hessian sacks, to wrap up plants against the weather, or simply move them under cover.

HOW TO CHOOSE CROP PROTECTION

The crop protection that is right for you depends on what you want to grow, and when. A cold frame is ideal for starting seedlings early and hardening off plants, but it doesn't offer frost protection. A greenhouse or a polytunnel gives you enough indoor space to grow lots of tomatoes and cucumbers, but is a considerable investment, so you may prefer to stick to outdoor varieties.

Cloches and tunnels are perhaps the most versatile, as they come in a range of sizes and can easily be moved around as necessary. They're enough to keep you in winter salads through all but the most evil weather.

Pocket Tip 🐖

Try and inspect plant protection products before you buy them as some are difficult to assemble and others are simply too fragile to withstand allotment life.

WHICH CROPS TO GROW UNDER PROTECTION

Summer season

- **Tomatoes**. These are commonly grown in greenhouses and polytunnels.

- **Peppers and aubergines**. These are happy in a sunny spot, but more likely to ripen under cover.

- **Cucumbers**. Indoor varieties benefit from the high humidity in a greenhouse or polytunnel.

- **Carrots**. These benefit from fleece protection to stave off the carrot root fly.

- **Brassicas**. These can be kept under a fine mesh to defend them from cabbage caterpillars.

Pocket Tip 🛒

Pot up your favourite herbs (eg basil, mint and parsley) and pop them on the windowsill in autumn, to ensure fresh supplies right through until spring.

Autumn, winter and spring

- **Leafy vegetables**. Oriental brassicas, winter and spring cabbages, winter lettuce, lamb's lettuce, land cress and parsley can all be sown in late summer for harvesting through the autumn and winter. In an unheated greenhouse, or cloches, the plants chosen have to be fully hardy. The idea is to have tender crops throughout the winter or early spring harvests.

- **Carrots and peas**. These can be sown under cover in late winter for early spring harvests.

- **French beans**. A protected environment allows these tender plants to be sown earlier in spring than they would survive outside.

- **Strawberries**. Strawberries in pots can be brought into the greenhouse in midwinter, for early spring crops. Open the vents on sunny days to refresh the air and allow in pollinating insects, but remember to close them at night.

- **Broad beans**. Winter protection keeps broad beans safe from pigeons, and gives you an even earlier harvest.

Autumn and winter sowings of hardy annuals, biennials and perennials (including flowers) are more reliable when given some protection.

Pocket Tip 🛒

Crop protection is not enough to save tender plants from the winter weather; to ensure their survival bring them inside to a place that doesn't drop below freezing.

♛ SHEDS ♛

Once merely a hideaway for a hen-pecked husband, sheds have become an invaluable part of gardens and allotments.

WHY HAVE A SHED?

A garden shed tends to become a repository for all the junk that's too big, or too dirty, to fit into the house. But if you've been bitten by the gardening bug then it's time to clear some space, because a shed can come in very handy.

If your allotment site allows sheds you've struck gold because it means you can leave things behind, rather than having to carry tools backwards and forwards every time you visit.

STORAGE

A shed is a great place to store your tools, pots and other gardening sundries. Try to keep some semblance of order, or the contents rapidly descend into chaos! Adding pegs to the wall means you can hang tools up; a rack allows you to get the stacks of pots off the floor as well.

Pocket Tip 🛒

A shed is a great place to store bits and bobs in tins, but it's not a good place to store your seeds (due to the fluctuating temperatures) so take those home with you.

POTTING SHED/BOTHY

A shed with a window and a potting bench is a nice place to pot up plants and seedlings, particularly if you have a view over the plot and can ruminate over what needs doing outside. It's also a nice haven from the rain or cold wind.

Pocket Fact 🏷

A bothy is a traditional gardener's shelter.

SUMMER HOUSE

In Europe and Scandinavia it's common for allotments to have large sheds that are more like summer houses or cabins (complete with furniture and cooking facilities) so that families can spend the weekend on their plot. There are one or two spectacular sheds here in the UK, too, but it's more common to have something smaller. If your lease permits it there's no reason why you can't keep a BBQ and folding chairs inside – add a veranda, and treat yours like a beach hut!

DRYING SPACE

At the end of the growing season you may have onions and garlic, or beans, that need to be properly dried before they can be stored. As long as your shed is dry, and not too stuffy, it's good enough to do the job. Once your crop is dry, though, you need to take it home to provide it with the best possible storage conditions, as sheds get very cold in winter.

RESOURCE COLLECTION

A shed takes up a lot of space, so you may feel it needs to work hard to warrant it. Adding guttering to your shed means that you can use it to collect rainwater, and if you want a light inside, you could even put a small solar panel on the roof.

VERTICAL SPACE

You can also use your shed as a support for climbing plants. Depending on what you want to grow, you may need to attach a trellis, or put up plant wires at strategic intervals.

HOW TO CHOOSE A SHED

Sheds can be expensive, so it's important to ensure yours meets your needs.

Size

The first consideration is what size of shed you want. Is it primarily for storage, or do you want a potting shed or summer house?

On an allotment site there may be restrictions on how large your shed can be, but in a garden it's more about aesthetics and how much of your garden you can spare.

Pocket Fact ✎

Garden sheds don't normally need planning permission, as long as they don't take up more than half the garden, aren't too tall, and are far enough from the road. Your allotment lease should detail the policy on sheds. For more information, see the government's Planning Portal website (www.planningportal.gov.uk) or check with your local council.

Cost

Prices for flat-pack wooden sheds start at around £150 (plastic and metal sheds are more expensive). You will need to assemble it yourself and ensure a suitable base is present to build upon. Concrete paving slabs are a popular choice, but make sure that they're level.

If you can be flexible about the size and design, it's possible to get second-hand sheds (even free ones, via Freegle), which you can dismantle and transport yourself. If you're handy you could also collect recycled materials to build your own structure.

Design

If you want a potting shed, it needs to have a window unless you plan to install a light. You'll also need enough height to stand up straight, and enough space to move around once you've installed your potting bench. A storage-only shed can be simpler.

Pocket Tip 🖑

You may want to add some wildlife-friendly features to your shed. It's possible to add a green roof that grows plants for wildlife, or you could raise the shed off the ground and turn the space into a wildlife haven with air bricks and hollow stems to provide habitats. An internet search for 'wildlife stack' will turn up plenty of inspiration.

♛ SEED SUPPLIERS ♛

The main seed companies all have ranges that are available through garden centres, mail order, or online:

- Thompson & Morgan (www.thompson-morgan.com)
- Mr Fothergill's (www.mr-fothergills.co.uk)
- Suttons (www.suttons.co.uk)
- Dobies (www.dobies.co.uk)
- Kings Seeds (offers discounts to allotment societies and groups, and NSALG members) (www.kingsseeds.com)
- D.T. Brown (www.dtbrownseeds.co.uk)
- The Organic Gardening Catalogue (www.organiccatalog.com)
- Marshalls (www.marshalls-seeds.co.uk)

Most seed companies also offer a range of fruit and vegetable plants. There are other, smaller, seed companies, which can be turned up with a quick internet search. Many also advertise in gardening magazines.

♛ DIY EQUIPMENT ♛

Gardening doesn't have to be an expensive hobby. There are plenty of tools and sundries that make the job easier, but you can avoid spending a fortune by buying second-hand, or making your own.

Pocket Tip 🛒

You may find second-hand tools offered in local second hand shops, or classified ads. You can also buy them via the Preloved website (www.preloved.co.uk) or eBay.

MAKE YOUR OWN

- You can fashion your own large dibber by paring down the end of a broken spade handle – it makes short work of planting out leeks.

- Turn a tin or container with a plastic lid into a string dispenser – make a hole and poke the end through for dry and tangle-free string.

- Cold frames can be made from unwanted windows.

- Plastic bottles make great cloches, particularly if you can find a source of the large bottles used in water coolers (which have to be regularly replaced for hygiene reasons).

- Old hessian sacks are great for storing potatoes, and for protecting tender plants and terracotta pots in winter.

- Net curtains are great for keeping pests off of your veggies – so much so that you may have trouble finding any in your local charity shop!

- The plastic trays you get from the supermarket make great little seed trays, and clean yoghurt pots are great for potting on seedlings.

- Cut up plastic milk bottles (or even old blinds) for plant labels, and use a pencil or indelible marker. Or paint and use wooden offcuts, or stones, for a more attractive option.

- The small plastic bottles that probiotic drinks come in are perfect for cane toppers, which protect your eyes when you're bending over.

GROW YOUR OWN

Make space for some useful plants on your plot to save yourself some money.

- The fibrous leaves of the perennial New Zealand flax (*Phormium tenax*) make great plant ties. If you're trying to get on top of your weeds then bindweed also makes good twine!

- Bamboo is commonly used for plant supports, and you can grow your own; it's a vigorous and ornamental plant, but it can get a little invasive. Hazel and willow are other options. Have a look at the Allotment Forestry website (www.allotmentforestry.com/fact/growown.htm) for ideas.

- Adding a comfrey plant gives you a supply of leaves for making liquid feeds (simply steep them in water until they stink!) or a compost activator. 'Bocking 14' is a sterile variety that doesn't self-seed. You can also use nettles, if you have a patch. Or simply drown pesky weeds in a bucket for two to three weeks until they're dead, and put them to work feeding your crops.

- If you have a sunny spot and are up for a challenge, you can even try growing your own pot scrubbers – luffa seeds are available from several UK seed suppliers.

♛ USEFUL CONTACTS ♛ AND SUPPLIERS

Garden supplies are easily found at a garden centre, or in the gardening section of a local DIY store. If you want to shop online (or mail order) for a bigger selection, the following suppliers are well known and reliable:

- **Organic Gardening Catalogue** (www.organiccatalog.com). This is an invaluable resource if you want to garden organically. Not only does it sell seeds and plants, but it also has tools, sundries and fertilisers that are suitable for use by organic gardeners.

- **Harrod Horticultural** (www.harrodhorticultural.com). This offers a large range of tools and accessories for gardens of all sizes, including raised bed kits, polytunnels and small greenhouses.

- **Two Wests & Elliott's** (www.twowests.co.uk). This catalogue contains a lot of kit for more professional growers, but is still a useful resource for keen amateurs.

- **Hen & Hammock** (www.henandhammock.co.uk). This has a stylish range of garden supplies, many of which are ethically sourced or made from recycled materials.

- **Green Shopping Catalogue** (www.green-shopping.co.uk). This has plenty of useful tools for eco-conscious gardeners, as well as an amazing array of helpful books.

- **Crocus** (www.crocus.co.uk). This has a nice selection of wheelbarrows and trolleys, as well as plants, sundries and water butts.

- **Wiggly Wigglers** (www.wigglywigglers.co.uk). This has a large range of composters, bird food and gardening gear, including some reclaimed vintage items.

Pocket Tip

Most seed and plant catalogues (see p. 57 for more contact details) also feature a small selection of garden sundries, so you can save the postage and add what you need to one big order.

♛ HEALTH AND SAFETY ♛

According to ROSPA (the Royal Society for the Prevention of Accidents), around 300,000 people go to hospital every year after being injured in the garden. Of those, over a third are children, and 87,000 are injured while actively gardening, or doing garden DIY. With a little forethought, and the right safety equipment, you can drastically reduce the risks.

GLOVES

Although there are benefits to getting your hands dirty, and jobs that are easier with bare hands, a good pair of gardening gloves protects your hands from prickles and wear-and-tear and is recommended when you're handling compost.

MASKS

Compost heaps are a breeding ground for fungi, and can be full of fungal spores. They're vital to the rotting process, and usually harmless, but a dry compost heap can also be the source of a lot of dust. You may wish to wear a mask when digging out your compost, or damp it down to keep dust to a minimum. Stand upwind of the compost, so it doesn't blow in your face.

If you're using a strimmer to clear your plot then wear protective goggles to protect your eyes.

BOOTS

It's common for people to garden in sandals and flip-flops in the summer, but if you're wielding a spade or fork then you should wear sturdy boots to protect your toes. A new allotment, potentially the site of numerous unpleasant surprises, is also the place for sturdy footwear. Suitable shoes will also prevent slips and falls on muddy ground or slippery paths.

KNEE PADS

Knee protection is very useful on stony or cold ground, and also helps to keep your clothes clean. You can get a traditional kneeling pad, or knee pads which strap on over your trousers.

Top ten safety tips

1. *Always wash your hands thoroughly after gardening, and keep open wounds covered or wear gloves.*
2. *If you have children and pets, make sure you can recognise potentially poisonous garden and wild plants. If you have a pond on your allotment then cover it over or fence it in to prevent children from falling in. You should make sure there's a way for wildlife to get out, too.*
3. *Ensure garden chemicals, even organic ones, are stored safely and away from children and always follow the manufacturer's instructions when using them. Wear the right protective gear, and apply the chemicals at the right time of day and in the right weather, to protect your health and that of your neighbours and the environment. Don't store liquids in fizzy pop bottles if there's a risk of confusion about the contents.*
4. *Store tools properly – stepping on a rake is only funny in cartoons. Tidying the hosepipe away saves you from tripping, and makes it last longer.*

5. When working with power tools, use a safety device to ensure it cuts out if there's a problem.

6. Be careful with fires and BBQs (see p. 44 for more tips).

7. Use cane toppers to cover the tops of canes, to protect your eyes.

8. Pot shards are often recommended as a base layer in flower pots, to improve drainage. In practice they are unnecessary and can lead to nasty cuts when plants are repotted.

9. Long sleeves and trousers may seem unnecessary in the summer, but they are a great barrier against scratches and bites; tuck your trousers into your socks in long grass.

10. Try doing some gentle warm-up exercises before doing anything strenuous, to minimise aches and pains.

FIRST AID KIT

A first aid kit is always a handy thing to have around, whether you're gardening at home or on an allotment. Keep it handy in the bathroom, the shed or even in the car. Your allotment site may also have its own kit, and even trained first aiders.

Pocket Tip

Check your kit regularly to make sure your supplies are all there and are still within their use-by date.

You can buy a ready-made first aid kit, or put together your own in a watertight plastic case. Good thing to include are:

• Plasters in varying shapes and sizes, or a roll of sticking plaster and a pair of scissors

• Sterile gauze dressings, individually packed

• Micropore tape

• A bandage and safety pins

- Disposable gloves
- Antiseptic wipes and hand sanitiser
- Tweezers
- Insect bite cream or spray
- Painkillers
- Instant ice packs

Pocket Fact

St John Ambulance can be hired to provide first aid cover for allotment events, and its website (www.sja.org.uk/sja/default.aspx) gives basic first aid information.

6

WHAT TO GROW AND HOW TO GROW IT

Even a quick look at a seed catalogue can leave you feeling bombarded with information. There are so many different plants you could grow, and each one comes in numerous varieties with a delicious description that's enough to make your mouth water. In this chapter we look at how to narrow down the choices to a good list of crops for you to grow, and outline the different methods you can employ to grow these crops.

♛ WHAT TO GROW ♛

IN A BIG SPACE

With a big space your options are nearly limitless, but the trick is to fill it in a way that covers the ground, keeps weed problems at bay and provides harvests for much of the year, without producing gluts.

The nice thing about having a large plot is that it allows you to grow vegetables that need a lot of room and also those that take up space for a very long time.

Most people eat a lot of potatoes, and turning a sizeable bed over to spuds will give you a valuable harvest you can store over the winter. Pumpkins and winter squash are large, sprawling plants. Again, they produce a harvest that can feed you (if you choose the right varieties) well into next year. As each sweetcorn plant only produces one or two cobs, you also need plenty of space to grow a sizeable sweetcorn crop.

Pocket Tip 🌾

Mini-sweetcorn plants are just as big; it's only the cobs that are smaller!

The vegetables that spend a lot of time in the ground also tend to be the ones ready for harvest in early spring, during the 'hungry gap' when it's difficult to produce a harvest without proper planning. Leeks, sprouting broccoli, winter cabbages, Brussel sprouts, leeks and Jerusalem artichokes are all sown or planted early in one year to be harvested early in the next – tying up space for an entire year.

Pocket Tip 🌾

If you miss sowing winter vegetables in spring, buy them as small plants around midsummer.

If you plan to garden the same plot for years to come, a large plot also allows you to devote space to perennial vegetables, many of which are gourmet treats but have a very short season. Consider globe artichokes, asparagus and rhubarb.

And if your allotment lease allows it, you could plant fruit and nut trees.

IN A SMALL SPACE

With careful planning a small space can be very productive, but you do have to choose your plants carefully. Do they offer enough reward for the space they take up?

In small plots, the plants that come into their own are the ones that quickly produce a harvest, and if they keep doing so over a long time then that's ideal. Salad and stir-fry crops come into this category – lettuces and oriental leaves, radishes, baby beetroot and carrots. Look for 'cut-and-come-again' leaves that can be harvested over several weeks.

It also pays to think in 3D. Do you have any vertical spaces that plants could grow up? A wall, fence or trellis could be the perfect spot for peas or climbing beans, scrambling mini-squashes or even a well-trained fruit bush.

Pocket Tip

Underplanting fruit trees and bushes with alpine strawberries gives two crops from the same space.

IN CONTAINERS

The restricted root space of containers means that they are not suitable for some plants, but there are plenty that will thrive in a pot.

Plant quick leafy crops (lettuce, leaf beet, spinach, spring onions) in small pots, or you could try alpine strawberries. Larger pots are good for tomatoes, peppers and dwarf beans. In large containers you can plant dwarf fruit trees and courgettes.

Many herbs are also happy in containers, and make good use of the space.

Pocket Tip

Have fresh seedlings ready to replant in your containers as soon as one harvest is ready.

BY PLOT TYPE

What type of plot you have also affects which crops you should choose. An urban allotment will have restrictions, and you may not want to invest in expensive perennial plants on a plot you don't own. It may also be vulnerable to vandals and thieves.

If your plot is close to farmland then rural pests such as rabbits may make a meal out of your leafy crops, and an exposed location may make life difficult for tender plants.

A garden (whether it's yours or not) is usually a protected space where prized plants will be safe and there's easy access to water for thirsty crops. A 'borrowed' space of any kind brings uncertainty – you may have to move on before long-lived plants become fruitful.

Pocket Tip 🛒

If your plot is in a public space then plan for more losses, so you can stay calm when passers-by help themselves.

♛ METHODS TO MAKE THE MOST ♛ OF YOUR SPACE

Whatever space you have, there are various techniques that help you make the most of it. Some are very simple; others take a bit of planning.

INTERCROPPING

Intercropping aims to grow two crops from the same piece of ground. It takes advantage of differing plant needs. The classic example is the 'Native American Three Sisters', where the stalks of sweetcorn plants are used to support a crop of climbing beans, and a squash scrambles underneath as a ground cover to keep the soil surface cool and damp. For intercropping to work you need to match the plants correctly and to have healthy soil. For the Three Sisters you also have to sow each type of seed at the right time, so that the corn is tall enough to support the beans, and the beans are tall enough not to be swallowed by the squash plants. This is a bit too tricky for novice gardeners, but can be a useful method once you have a bit more experience.

UNDERCROPPING

Undercropping is the planting of a low-growing crop under a taller one. Alpine strawberries are nice under fruit trees, and low-growing herbs and flowers around fruit bushes can act as a living mulch and attract pollinating insects to improve your fruit crop. In the height of the summer, leafy vegetables such as lettuce and spinach also benefit from being planted in the shade of taller plants.

CATCH-CROPPING

If you clear one crop and it's not time to plant the next one planned for that space then you can sow a catch crop – a quick-growing vegetable that will be harvested before you need the space. Salad leaves and radishes are typical catch crops.

Pocket Fact ⬥

Pests and diseases are always worse in cramped conditions, so don't try to fit too much into your space.

CUT-AND-COME-AGAIN

Some leafy vegetables (many lettuces and cabbages) form hearts and are harvested once. With cut-and-come-again vegetables you harvest a few leaves from each plant at a time, and it provides a crop over several weeks. Look for loose-leaf lettuces, salad mixes and oriental vegetables, as well as leaf beet, chard and spinach.

It's also possible to use one vegetable for two crops. Take a few leaves from beetroots or turnips, then leave the plant in place to harvest the roots later. Or eat some of the fresh tips of your pea plants as peashoots.

Pocket Tip ⬥

Overharvesting cut-and-come-again crops will cause them to finish early, so don't overdo it.

SUCCESSIONAL SOWING

If you sow a long row of lettuce seeds then they will all be ready to harvest at the same time. The same is true of radishes, beet-root and carrots, spring onions and oriental greens. Sow short rows (a pinch or two of seeds) instead, every couple of weeks throughout the season, for staggered harvests and no gluts.

SQUARE FOOT GARDENING

Square foot gardening was developed in America, and involves using raised beds divided into squares – each one is one square foot, hence the name. A different crop is planted into each square (the number of plants in each square depends on the final size of the plant) and each square is harvested and then immediately replanted with a different crop. Square foot gardening reduces the work involved in gardening, eliminates gluts and takes care of rotations for you. It also allows you to grow a large variety of plants, year-round, in a very small space.

Pocket Tip

Sow seeds in trays or modules to help with successional sowing or square foot gardening, then plant them out when you have spare space.

STACKING

Plants in a natural forest grow in different ways to make the best use of available light. Some hug the ground; others aim for the sky. Roots burrow down and climbers hitch a ride. Stacking involves putting different plants with different growing habits in the same place, as they would grow in nature. A forest garden is a garden designed along these lines, with plants (mainly perennial) occupying all the available ecological niches. The result is a productive and low-maintenance, but rather unconventional, plot.

Catalogue jargon

There are a few terms you'll see in catalogues and seed packets which you'll need to be aware of for successful growing.

__F1:__ a plant variety with F1 in its name is a hybrid between two different parents. All of the seeds in the packet will grow into *almost identical plants, which all crop at the same time and are usually very vigorous. F1 are not good varieties to choose if you want to save your own seeds (see p. 139 for more details).*

__Male or female:__ flowers have male and female sex organs. Some plants have flowers that contain both sex organs, while on others all of the flowers will be male or female, and so the plant is called male or female. For some fruits and vegetables there are advantages to having all male or all female plants, rather than a mixture.

♛ SEASONAL GROWING ♛

INTRODUCTION TO SEASONS

The UK has a temperate climate, with four seasons. Each season can be divided into three growing periods, although the exact timing of these periods will depend on your local climate: for example spring arrives later as you travel north, and each year is different.

Month	Season	Gardening period
January	Winter	Mid winter
February	Winter	Late winter
March	Spring	Early spring
April	Spring	Mid spring
May	Spring	Late spring
June	Summer	Early summer
July	Summer	Mid summer
August	Summer	Late summer
September	Autumn	Early autumn
October	Autumn	Mid autumn
November	Autumn	Late autumn
December	Winter	Early winter

WHAT TO GROW WHEN

All crops have an ideal growing period. For most annuals this means they are sown in spring and harvested in summer. Hardy crops may be sown in spring, late summer or autumn, to grow through the winter.

Other crops need the winter cold to grow properly. Apple trees expect to be cold over winter (in hotter climates they grow different varieties), and garlic likes to put down roots in chilly soil.

Many oriental vegetables are sensitive to the day length (because the come from a different part of the world) and are best grown after midsummer – sown earlier they tend to flower too quickly.

See pp76–123 for general advice for each vegetable, or look at the Growing Calendar at the back of the book. If you're sowing seeds then check the seed packet for the ideal sowing time for the variety you've chosen.

Pocket Tip

Don't slavishly follow gardening advice if it's not right for your weather. Wait until the conditions are right for your plants' needs.

♛ COMPANION PLANTING ♛

Companion planting is about pairing plants in the hope that they grow better together than they would apart. Most of the information on the subject is anecdotal; there hasn't been a great deal of scientific research. In fact, it is a very complicated subject, as there are many factors that could positively affect plant growth and combinations on one plot but not on another.

INTERACTIONS

There are many ways in which plants can interact, some are positive and some are negative, so it's up to you to decide if the advantages of companion planting will win over on your plot.

Positive interactions

- **Microclimates**. Larger plants (such as sweetcorn or fruit bushes) may provide shelter or shade to smaller plants (eg lettuce).

- **Soil improvement**. Some plants (such as beans) can add nitrogen to the soil. Others have tough roots, which break up soil and allow other plant roots to penetrate.

- **Confusing pests**. Many pests (such as the carrot fly) are attracted by the smell of their target plant, but can be confused by different scents.

- **Trapping pests**. Some plants (such as nasturtiums and lettuce) attract pests so well they can be used as trap crops.

- **Attracting insects**. Flowering plants attract pollinating and beneficial insects.

- **Mulches**. Low-growing plants (such as strawberries) keep the soil damp and cool for taller ones.

Pocket Tip

Chamomile is such a good companion that it is known as the doctor plant as it improves the health of plants nearby.

Negative interactions

- **Competition**. Some plants are too vigorous to play well with others, and rapidly crowd them out.

- **Allelopathy**. Some plants produce chemicals that prevent others from growing, or seeds from germinating. The effect is sometimes useful (for example Hungarian grazing rye is a green manure that discourages weed growth) but often the production of chemicals can be harmful to other plants.

- **Hosting disease**. Some weeds are notorious for hosting disease and passing it on to your crops. Keep wild areas away from your vegetable beds.

Only experience and experimentation can tell you which plants are 'good companions' in your garden, but as a start you can try the following:

- Use chives and onions to hide the smell of carrots from the carrot fly.

- Pair up tomatoes with basil or marigolds to repel whitefly.

♛ TIPS ON FIGHTING PESTS ♛ AND DISEASES

Attacks by pests and diseases can be very demoralising for any gardener, but you can minimise the problems by looking after your plants and your soil. Check the plant profiles in the next chapter to see which pests and diseases to be on the look out for, and deal with problems quickly.

Top ten tips to keep your plot healthy

1. *Start with the soil. Healthy soil leads to healthy plants with fewer problems. Make compost, and use it.*
2. *Follow a crop rotation (even a simple one) to prevent the build-up of problems.*
3. *Be vigilant. Most problems are easily dealt with early on.*
4. *Keep plants healthy. Feed and water as required, and don't over-crowd them.*
5. *Traps and barriers work for many pests (such as slugs, snails and caterpillars). Removal by hand works for many others.*
6. *If the pests threaten to take over, look for a biological control (a natural predator) that you can introduce before you reach for the pesticide (which will disrupt the balance and make things worse in the long run).*
7. *Environmentally friendly pesticides are available for slugs and sap-sucking insects such as aphids.*

8. Grow a wide variety of plants. Big blocks of one plant allow pests and diseases to find their host plants with ease.

9. When choosing plants and seeds, look for varieties that are disease-resistant.

10. Diseased plants should be removed and thrown away, not composted.

Pocket Tip 🖎

Pest and disease problems vary from year to year, so it's worth trying again next year even if you have problems.

IDENTIFYING GOOD AND BAD BUGS

It used to be that the only good bug was a dead bug, but the growth of organic gardening and the removal of many pesticides from sale is making us look again at our insects.

Bad bugs

In general, the bugs that eat plants are slow-moving.

- Woodlice have a bad reputation but generally only munch plants that have already been damaged by other creatures. They love decaying plant material, so remove old crops to the compost heap.

- Slugs and snails leave obvious trails; look for them in damp nooks and crannies. Remove them by hand, drown them in shallow trays of beer or employ cloches to keep seedlings safe.

- Under cover, the biggest pest is red spider mite. The mites themselves are tiny, but the webbing they make is obvious, as are the damaged leaves. Spraying plants with water to raise the humidity discourages spider mites. A biological control is available if you have a serious problem.

- In pots look for vine weevil damage – the adults cut semi-circles from the edges of leaves, but the larvae eat roots.

Squash slow-moving adults as you see them, then use a biological control to eradicate their larvae.

The most damaging pests are also the most common and the easiest to identify. Keep an eye out for them when you visit your plot – most are easily dealt with if found early.

Good bugs

Although your basic instinct may be to get rid of all bugs, there are some bugs that can be of benefit to your allotment and your plants.

- **Ladybirds**. These are easily identifiable. Ladybird larvae look scary (like tiny black crocodiles with orange patches) but they're only interested in eating aphids. Ladybirds hibernate through the winter in the untidy bits of the garden.

- **Lacewings**. These have graceful green wings and sometimes come inside for the winter. They also love munching on aphids.

- **Hoverflies**. These look like little wasps, but are smaller and hover around flowers. They are good pollinators, and their offspring eat aphids.

- **Spiders**. These are unpopular, but very good at catching and eating all kinds of insect pests.

Pocket Tip 🛒

A bug viewer is a useful tool – it allows you to capture and magnify those creepy-crawlies.

7

CROP PROFILES

Now that we've covered the different methods you can employ for growing your own produce we'll look at profiles of the different vegetables, fruit and herbs you can grow on your allotment.

♛ VEGETABLES ♛

ASPARAGUS

- Asparagus is a perennial plant. The asparagus season is short; plants have to be allowed to grow new leaves to feed themselves.

- The plants are only suitable for growing in the ground, on large plots.

Pocket Fact 🗡
The white asparagus spears popular in Europe are blanched (whitened) by covering them in soil. Lack of light prevents the spears from turning green.

Grow

- Seeds are sown outside, where you want them to grow, in April and May.

- You can also buy one year-old 'crowns' (roots) to plant out in March and April.

- Choose an F1 variety with all-male plants if you want a uniform harvest. If you have the space, plant more than one variety; they mature at slightly different times, giving an extended harvest. Plants grown from seed will be mixed sexes and the size of the spears will vary.

- The choice of variety is limited with seeds, and your first harvest a year later, but the cost is much lower.

- An asparagus bed is productive for years, so prepare the soil properly beforehand – plants like well-drained soil with plenty of organic matter.

- To plant crowns, dig a hole 20cm (8 inches) deep, then make a 10cm (4 inches) mound of soil down the middle. The crowns are spread over the mound, 30cm (1 foot) apart, and then covered in soil. A surface mulch helps keep the soil moist and weed-free.

Harvest

- Your first (small) harvest will be in three years (from seed) or two (from crowns), with full harvests in future years.

- The harvest period is from May until midsummer. Harvest all spears that appear, as once they unfurl the harvest is finished. From midsummer onwards, allow the plant to grow naturally.

Problems

- Asparagus beetles need to be picked off by hand. The larvae are dark-coloured caterpillars; the adults have a red head and black and white patterned bodies.

- Composting the ferns once they die back in winter helps.

AUBERGINES

- Aubergines are beautiful plants with large hairy leaves and pretty flowers, but the stems can be prickly.

- They grow well in a container on a sheltered patio, or in a greenhouse or polytunnel.

- You could also try a sunny windowsill – aubergines love sunshine.

Grow

- Aubergine seeds and plants are widely available, but choose your variety carefully.

- 'Early' varieties are more likely to fruit reliably in our climate.

- Larger fruits take longer to grow and are riskier.

- Sow seeds indoors in February and March.

- Keep plants inside (repotting as necessary) until the risk of frost has passed planting outside in late May or early June.

- Keep plants well watered, and give tomato feed (rich in potassium) when they flower and fruit.

Harvest

- Aubergines are harvested in late summer.

- Harvest them when they are plump and the skin is shiny (their mature size depends on variety).

- Leaving them too long will make the fruit increasingly bitter.

Problems

- Red spider mites are a problem. Mist the plants with water regularly to keep the humidity high.

- Aubergines don't fruit well in poor summers.

Pocket Fact ❧

Modern varieties of aubergine have been bred to be far less bitter.

BEETROOT

- Beetroot is usually grown for the roots, but the leaves are also edible.

- 'Baby' varieties are good in containers.

- Long-rooted varieties are most suited to sandy and well-cultivated soils.

Grow

- 'Boltardy' is a popular variety because it is less prone to flowering before forming roots.

- 'Chioggia' is an old Italian variety that grows concentric pink and white rings.

- Sow beetroot seeds where you want them to grow, from April to July, in small batches.

- Keep well watered.

- For baby beetroot leave seedlings in small clusters.

- For large roots thin seedlings to 8cm (3 inches) apart.

Pocket Fact

Beetroot 'seeds' are actually fruit clusters, from which several seedlings grow.

Harvest

- Beetroots should be ready to pick between August and November.

- Unless you want to store them for winter, beetroot are best harvested and eaten young, as baby beets.

- Baby leaves can be added to salads; large leaves can be used like chard.

- Sow extra if you want to eat both leaves and roots, as harvesting too many leaves prevents good roots from forming.

- Any seedlings you thin out can also be eaten.

- Twist the stems to remove leaves from harvested beetroot – if you cut them, the roots will 'bleed'.

Problems

- Roots go 'woody' in dry conditions.

- If beet leaf miner attacks, remove and compost affected leaves.

BROAD BEANS

- Broad beans are very hardy, providing a harvest earlier in the year than French and runner beans.

- Broad beans are happiest growing in the ground, although dwarf varieties can be grown in a large container.

- It is not a productive crop in small spaces.

Grow

- Broad beans can be sown either in November, to overwinter, or in February. Soil that remains waterlogged over winter should not be used for a winter sowing.

- Sow seeds in double rows, so the beans support each other. Space each pair of rows around 20cm (8 inches) apart. Beans can also be sown in small pots or modules, and planted out later.

- When the beans reach their full height (which depends on variety), snip off the leafy tops to discourage blackfly. You can eat these as a cooked green.

- Broad beans can take nitrogen from the air, with the help of soil bacteria, so they don't need feeding as they grow.

Harvest

- Broad beans should be ready for harvest in June and July.

- Autumn-sown beans arrive earlier than those sown in spring.

- Young pods can be cooked and eaten whole, like mangetout.

- As the beans become more pronounced, they need shelling like peas.

- As the beans get larger still, they develop a 'skin' – blanch them in boiling water and squeeze them out of this tough skin to make them more tempting.

- When the plants are finished, chop them down and leave the roots in the soil, where any spare nitrogen feeds the next crop.

Problems

- If blackflies attack the plant, remove the leafy tops. Sowing in November also helps.

- Mice may take seeds before they germinate; you can sow the seeds in modules and transplant if this is a problem.

- Chocolate spot is a fungal disease that's worse in cool, damp conditions. Space plants far enough apart to allow air to circulate between.

Pocket Fact

Broad bean flowers are edible (add them raw to salads) and an early source of nectar for bees.

BROCCOLI

- The green 'broccoli' sold in supermarkets is known to growers as calabrese.

- Purple sprouting broccoli comes early in the year and forms small sprouts over several weeks rather than one big head.

- Summer sprouting broccoli provides a harvest in one season.

- Broccoli and calabrese are not suited to containers, or small spaces, due to their size and long growing time.

- For smaller plots consider kailaan (Chinese broccoli) or raab (related to turnips), which offer a similar harvest from smaller plants much more quickly.

Pocket Fact 🔖

Broccoli is made up of clusters of flower buds. Harvest the heads before the yellow flowers start to open.

Grow

- Sow calabrese indoors in April, for planting out in May, or sow outside in May.

- Sow purple sprouting broccoli inside in February and March, or outside in April and May. Plant out by the end of June.

- Sow summer sprouting broccoli outside from April through to June.

- Space plants at least 30cm (1 foot) apart.

- Keep plants well watered.

- Purple sprouting broccoli plants are tall and need staking in autumn to prevent them being rocked by the winter winds, which leads to root damage.

Harvest

- Harvest calabrese heads from June to the end of August.

- Harvest flower shoots from summer sprouting broccoli as soon as they begin to appear in June. Keep removing them, as once the plant flowers the harvest stops.

- The harvest season doesn't end until October, but you need to stagger your sowings – each plant crops for a few weeks.

- Purple sprouting broccoli plants stay in the ground for a whole year; harvest them the following April and May. As for summer sprouting, keep removing the shoots before they flower.

Problems

- Club root is an incurable, soil-borne disease; buy plants from reputable suppliers, and if you visit other gardens wash the mud from your boots.

- Pigeons attack overwintering plants, but can be kept away with nets.

- Cabbage white butterflies are a problem during the summer months. Pick off caterpillars as you see them, or cover all plants with horticultural fleece or a small-gauge net *before* you see the butterflies on the wing.

- Brassicas are fussy about soil pH; check yours to see whether you need to add garden lime before planting.

CABBAGE

- With a little bit of planning, and plenty of space, it's possible to have cabbages growing on your plot year-round.

- Spring cabbages are followed by summer cabbages, then autumn and winter cabbages (including stunning red cabbages).

- Cabbages are large plants and take up space for a long time – they're best grown on allotments and big plots.

- In smaller gardens, stick to Chinese cabbage and other Oriental leafy vegetables.

Pocket Fact

Couve tronchuda *(Portuguese cabbage or kale) is an old-fashioned, dual-purpose vegetable. The leaves are eaten like cabbage, and the thick leaf mid-ribs are cooked up as a separate dish.*

Grow

- Summer cabbages are sown indoors in February and March, or outside in March and April.

- Autumn cabbages are sown at the same time, and winter cabbages a month later.

- Spring cabbages and Chinese cabbage are sown in July and August.

- Sow seeds in pots and modules, then plant your seedlings out about six weeks later, at the spacing recommended for the varieties you have chosen.

- Keep your plants well watered, so that they grow at a steady rate.

- Cabbages won't form good, solid hearts unless they're happy.

Harvest

- Cabbages are ready to harvest once they have formed a solid heart of a size you're happy with.

- Simply use a knife or your secateurs to cut the head free.

- You can also harvest some on a cut-and-come-again basis, so you have a steady supply of leaves. (Either harvest leaves or wait for heads; you can't have both.)

Problems

- You're likely to encounter the same problems as for broccoli (see p.81).

Pocket Tip

When you harvest spring and summer cabbages, leave a short stem in the ground and use a knife to cut a cross in the top. A second crop of baby cabbages will then grow from the stem and give you another harvest from the same space.

CARROTS

- Carrots can fit into every plot but they can be tricky. They're very intolerant of being overfed and of clumpy soil – both of which give them odd-shaped roots.

- Round- and short-rooted varieties are best for heavy or stony soil, and in containers.

- Early varieties are also good in small spaces, as they crop more quickly.

Pocket Fact

Carrots weren't originally orange, and it's now possible to grow carrots that are white, yellow, red, purple and black.

Grow

- Sow carrot seeds where you want them to grow, from April through to July (early carrot varieties can be sown in February and March).

- You'll need to thin your seedlings out to the required spacing, or your carrots won't produce roots.

- You can also buy seed tape, with seeds at the recommended spacing, which avoids thinning.

- They need to be kept well watered.

Harvest

- Harvest your carrots as soon as they're big enough to eat.

- You may need to brush the soil away from the tops of the roots to see whether their 'shoulders' have filled out.

- Harvest what you want, then water the rest to settle them back into the soil.

Problems

- The carrot root fly lays its eggs on the soil; the larvae burrow into carrots (and parsnips). They're at their worst in April/May and July/August, but they don't fly high, so a barrier around the crop can help, or you can use a fleece cover.

- Avoid touching the foliage unnecessarily – if you bruise any leaves, they will release the scent that attracts the carrot fly.

- There are also varieties of carrot with built-in resistance to carrot fly.

CAULIFLOWER

- Cauliflower is another vegetable that's difficult to grow well.

- Cauliflowers are best grown on allotments and large vegetable plots, as they're big plants and need space.

- Traditionally white, they're now available with green, orange and purple heads.

Pocket Fact

Romanesco broccoli is actually a variety of cauliflower. Its strange whorls are a natural fractal pattern.

Grow

- Summer cauliflowers are sown indoors from January to March, and planted out from March to May.

- Winter cauliflowers are sown from April to July, and planted out from July to October.

- Cauliflowers like to be firmly planted – it's one occasion when it's okay to step on your soil, so you can carefully tread them in.

- They also need a constant supply of food and water if they are to grow 'curds' properly, which means they need to be planted out at the correct spacing for the variety. If they're crowded, they won't grow well.

- Summer cauliflowers are harder to grow, because of the risk of drought and an increased tendency to flower too soon (called bolting).

Harvest

- In summer, harvest your cauliflower as soon as it forms a dense head of curds.

- In winter you can be more leisurely; bend the leaves over the head to keep the curds nice and clean, and harvest when you need them.

Problems

- Pest and disease problems are the same as for broccoli (see p.81).

CELERIAC

- Celeriac is a large, knobbly root with the same flavour as celery.

- It's very hardy, and doesn't need storage as it can be left in the ground until you need it.

Pocket Fact

When you harvest your celeriac root you can also use the stalks like celery.

Grow

- Seeds are sown indoors in February and March.

- Seedlings are planted out during May and June, about 40cm ($1\frac{1}{2}$ foot) apart.

- Celeriac doesn't need to grow in full sun, but it does need soil that stays moist throughout the summer.

Harvest

- Roots take several months to mature, so harvest time is from September through to March.

- If you want to store celeriac, remove the leaves.

Problems

- Slugs and snails love celeriac seedlings, so give them some protection until they're growing strongly.

CELERY

- Traditional celery varieties are planted into trenches, to blanch the stems.

- Modern varieties are self-blanching, making them easier on your back.

- In small gardens and containers try leaf celery or parcel. It grows like parsley, but the leaves taste like celery.

- The perennial herb lovage also tastes like celery.

Grow

- Sow seeds inside in February and March, then pot on the seedlings.

- Plant out after the risk of frost has passed in May and June.

- Space 30cm (1 foot) apart.

- Celery likes well-drained soil and a sunny spot, but also needs to be kept well watered.

Harvest

- Harvest plants from August to October, when the stems are large enough.

- Celery plants are not hardy and need to be harvested before the first frosts in autumn.

Problems

- Slugs and snails love the seedlings.

- Celery fly maggots are most problematic in April, so plant out celery in May.

Pocket Fact ⚲

Chinese celery is a strongly flavoured, thin-stemmed variety.

CHARD AND PERPETUAL SPINACH

- Chard and perpetual spinach (or leaf beet) are part of the beetroot family.

- Chard is around 30cm (1 foot) tall and has glossy green leaves with colourful midribs.

- Leaf beet is smaller and simply green.

- Both are useful, easy-to-grow leafy vegetables.

- Leaf beet is small enough to fit into any space, and both chard and leaf beet are happy in containers.

- Chard is pretty enough to squeeze into flower borders.

Pocket Fact ✎

Rainbow chard has a mix of leaf rib colours (white, yellow, orange and red) and is often grown as an ornamental edible.

Grow

- You can sow seeds in spring for summer harvests and in summer for autumn and winter.

- Plants may die back in harsh winter weather, but will regrow in milder periods.

- Chard and leaf beet are biennial plants, flowering in their second season.

- Removing the tall flower shoots can delay flowering, but it's best to have new seedlings waiting in the wings.

- Unfussy about soil and situation, these leafy crops are best when well watered and fed.

Harvest

- Regular harvesting promotes further leafy growth.

- Cut and use the older leaves first.

- Young leaf beet leaves can be added to salad; older leaves are best cooked.

- Chard leaves and stems are often cooked as separate vegetables.

Problems

- Beet leaf miners eat tunnels inside the leaves. Remove and compost affected leaves.

- Badly affected plants can be cut back to the ground; by the time they regrow the miners will have moved on.

COURGETTES, MARROWS, SQUASHES AND PUMPKINS

- Courgettes are young marrows, now seen as a summer staple.

- They are easy to grow – the main problem being coping with a glut.

- They do need space, but courgettes will be happy in a large pot if kept well watered and fed.

- Most varieties are bushy, but some clamber, which can be an advantage in a small space if you train them upwards.

- Pumpkins are winter squashes.

Pocket Fact ❧

Courgette and squash flowers are a delicacy, and there's even a courgette variety bred specifically for its flowers.

Grow

- Seeds are sown indoors in April, or outside in May.

- Plants can be put outside once the frosts have passed.

- Space 75cm ($2\frac{1}{2}$ feet) apart for courgettes and 100cm (3 feet) for squashes.

- Keep them well watered and well fed (they love rich soil).

Harvest

- Female courgette flowers have tiny fruits behind them, which rapidly turn into courgettes. If you want to eat courgette flowers, harvest the male ones, so that you don't miss out on any of the fruit.

- Harvest courgettes and summer squashes as and when they're large enough; they rapidly swell to marrows.

- Harvesting encourages more flowers and fruit to grow.

- Marrows and winter squashes are left to reach their full size (which depends on variety).

- To grow a giant pumpkin, limit the plant to just one or two fruits.

- To store squash, cut them with a T-shaped section of stem, but don't use it as a handle.

- Sit them in a warm place for a couple of weeks so that the skins cure nice and hard.

Problems

- As autumn approaches, all squash plants develop powdery mildew over the leaves.

- It's worse in dry weather, so watering helps, but simply shows the season is nearly over.

CUCUMBERS

- Cucumbers are climbing plants that belong to the courgette family.

- Some varieties prefer the warmth and humidity of a greenhouse, but there are outdoor varieties as well.

Pocket Fact ⚷

Columbus introduced cucumbers to the New World in 1494.

Grow

- Sow seeds indoors in April, for planting out in May and June.

- Plants will need a support to climb.

- Some varieties become bitter unless male flowers are removed; F1 varieties are often female only.

- Keep well watered, and feed with a high potash (tomato) feed when in flower and fruiting.

- Choose the right variety (indoor or outdoor) for your plot.

- As climbing plants, these make use of vertical space, and can be grown in containers if kept well watered and fed.

- 'Crystal Apple' is an interesting round variety.

Harvest

- Harvest fruits when they reach an acceptable size.

Problems

- Like squashes, cucumbers are prone to powdery mildew.

- Indoor plants may attract red spider mites.

- Regular watering helps prevent both.

Pocket Tip 🐾

If you can't eat a whole cucumber in one go, try leaving the fruit on the vine and cutting half off. The cut seals over and the remaining half stays much fresher than it would in the fridge!

FRENCH BEANS

- Slender green beans, borne on dwarf or climbing plants.

- Earlier and easier to grow than runner beans.

- French beans can be added to any plot: climbing plants can make use of vertical spaces, and dwarf plants are happy in containers.

- The choice of varieties is staggering, especially if you include heritage varieties.

Pocket Fact ⚒
'French' beans actually originated in Central America.

Grow

- Tender annuals, French beans are sown inside from March until July, for planting outside from May to August.

- As they are self-pollinating and don't need the attentions of insects, they can also be grown under cover for early and late crops.

- Dwarf varieties tend to crop over a short period, so sow a few seeds at a time over a few weeks to extend the harvest. Plants need to be 10cm (4 inches) apart in rows about 45cm ($1\frac{1}{2}$ feet) apart.

- Climbing varieties need tall supports, but offer smaller harvests over a longer period. They need to be about 30cm (1 foot) apart.

- French beans are legumes and won't need feeding in healthy soil, but benefit from being well watered.

Harvest

- Harvest the beans as soon as they're large enough, to encourage more to form.

- If you want to store dried beans over the winter, don't harvest from those plants as it will delay the formation of mature pods.

- If bad weather comes before the beans are dry, you can pull up the plants and hang them upside down inside to finish drying.

- It's easy to save some of your own seed for next year.

Problems

- Slugs are a problem for young plants.

- Older plants are susceptible to wind damage and benefit from a sheltered spot.

GARLIC

- Garlic is a root crop that belongs to the onion family.

- In Europe, soft-necked varieties are common.

- In the USA, hard-necked or 'serpent' garlic is more usual.

- Garlic isn't a fussy plant and can be grown anywhere.

- It will grow in containers, although the bulbs will be smaller than in the soil.

Pocket Fact 🔨

Elephant garlic, with its giant bulbs and milder flavour, is more closely related to leeks.

Grow

- Garlic is usually planted in November.

- To begin with, buy seed garlic from a reputable supplier. It is guaranteed disease-free and bred to grow in the British climate (unlike bulbs you may buy at the supermarket).

- From then on you can save your own bulbs for replanting, but don't break them up until the last minute as the cloves will dry out too much.

- Plant the largest cloves as they'll give you bigger bulbs.

- The final bulb size depends on spacing – leaving more space between cloves gives you larger bulbs.

- Average spacing is 15cm (6 inches).

- You may not see any signs of growth until February, depending on when you plant and the winter weather.

- There are also garlic varieties you can plant in spring.

- Plant the cloves the same way up as they were in the bulb.

- Keep your garlic bed well weeded, but don't water unless the weather is very dry as it can encourage rot.

- If you grow hard-necked garlic, it will form willowy 'scapes' in early summer, which are usually removed but could be eaten.

Harvest

- Garlic is ready to lift when the tops naturally die down, although you can dig up some early as 'green' garlic.

- To store garlic it needs to be 'cured' until the skins are papery dry. In wet weather this has to be done under cover.

- Hard-necked varieties don't store as well as soft-necked varieties, so eat those first, but keep a bulb or two back to plant out later.

Problems

- Garlic is usually trouble-free, but it can suffer from the same pests and diseases as onions (see p.100).

GLOBE ARTICHOKES

- Expensive to buy, globe artichokes are large perennial plants that are easy to grow.

- Globe artichokes are tall plants – up to 2m ($6\frac{1}{2}$ feet) – and need a permanent spot.

- They have ornamental value as well and are best in large gardens and on allotments.

Pocket Fact 🍴

Globe artichokes are thistles.

Grow

- Sow seeds in February and March, for planting out in May, 100cm (3 feet) apart.

- Your first harvest will be two years later.

- Plants grown from seed can be too spiny, so globe artichokes are often bought as plants.

- Replace plants every four to five years by planting out the offsets (baby plants) that grow at the base.

Harvest

- The flower heads can be harvested young, as baby artichokes, or just before the flowers open.

Problems

- Dry soil can lead to woody stems and flower heads that are dry and inedible.

- Very wet soil causes the plants to rot.

- Young artichoke plugs are susceptible to slug damage.

JERUSALEM ARTICHOKES

- Jerusalem artichokes are a tuber crop that resembles potatoes.

- They grow to 2m ($6\frac{1}{2}$ feet) tall and can be difficult to remove.

- Jerusalem artichokes can be grown successfully in containers, although yields are lower than in the ground.

- 'Fuseau' is a smooth variety that is easier to peel, but you can also plant out tubers bought for eating.

Pocket Fact ✎

Jerusalem artichokes are closely related to sunflowers.

Grow

- Choose your spot carefully, as it will be their permanent home.

- Plant tubers at least 30cm (1 foot) apart in early spring – they can go in from January until March.

- Plants make a good wind break as they mature, and may flower in September.

Harvest

- Wait until frost kills the tops before digging up the tubers.

- They store best in the ground, so dig them as you need them.

- Save some of your crop for replanting next year.

Problems

- Jerusalem artichokes are trouble-free, but unless you dig up all the tubers they will regrow next year and the clump may spread.

KALE

- Kale is the ultimate winter vegetable: very hardy and productive.

- Some kale varieties are ornamental, but they take up a lot of space and are in the ground for a long time; they aren't the best choice for containers or a small plot.

Pocket Fact ✎

Jersey kale (also known as giant cabbage or walking stick kale) can grow up to $5\frac{1}{2}$ m (18 feet) tall. Its stems used to be used for making walking sticks.

Grow

- Sow seeds outside in April and May.

- If you want to grow full-sized plants then they need to be at least 45cm ($1\frac{1}{2}$ feet) apart, but if you're growing them for cut-and-come-again salad (baby) leaves then space them closer.

- Large kale plants can be rocked by the wind in winter and may need staking on exposed plots.

Harvest

- Harvest baby leaves for salad, or leave plants to mature until they're needed in the winter months.

- Harvest the younger top leaves, rather than the older ones.

- Kale leaves are less bitter after a frost.

Problems

- Kale is less prone to pests and diseases than many other brassicas, but can suffer from the same problems as broccoli (see p.81).

- Overwintering plants may need to be netted to keep pigeons off.

LEEKS

- Another staple of the winter garden, leeks belong to the onion family.

- Grow on a small plot or in containers for a harvest of baby leeks.

- If you have an allotment then grow more than one variety to spread the harvest.

Pocket Fact ⚑

Leeks were part of the diet of ancient Egyptians.

Grow

- Sow seeds in March and April for planting outside in June and July.

- Use a dibber to make holes 20cm (8 inches) deep and drop a seedling into each one.

- Don't fill the holes, but water the seedlings well. This encourages a long, blanched white stem to form.

Harvest

- Harvest leeks as and when they're a useful size – as baby leeks or as mature plants.

- Loosen the soil around the roots before you pull them up.

Problems

- Leeks can suffer from the same pests and diseases as onions (see p.100) and garlic (see p.94).

- Leek rust is a fungal disease that causes orange spots on the leaves. Overcrowding and overfeeding make the problem worse. Check seed catalogues for resistant varieties.

- Leek moth larvae feed on leaves and stems. Remove them by hand, or grow plants under fleece.

LETTUCE, SPINACH AND SALAD LEAVES

- A large selection of salad leaves is now available, and the choice of lettuces is also immense.

- Salad crops are ideal anywhere, as they tuck in wherever there's space and are happy in containers.

Pocket Fact
Wild lettuce is used as a remedy for insomnia.

Grow

- Different varieties are best at different times of the year (it's possible to grow winter lettuce).

- Sow seeds in small batches to avoid gluts, then plant out the seedlings as space becomes available.

- Keep well watered in summer, or plants will flower quickly.

Harvest

- Harvest cut-and-come-again leaves once they are large enough.

- Lettuces that form dense hearts are cut once.

Problems

- Slugs and snails love lettuce.

- Plants can also be prone to fungal diseases if planted too closely together.

- Spinach tends to flower in dry weather.

ONIONS

- The workhorse of the kitchen – no vegetable plot should be without an onion or two.

- Onions don't take up much space and can be squeezed into most plots.

- Spring onions are a good container crop.

Pocket Fact
The onion has been recorded in history since 3000BC.

Grow

- Onions are usually grown from sets (small bulbs).

- Sets for maincrop onions are planted in March and April.

- For overwintering (Japanese) onions, sets are planted out in September and October.

- Standard spacing is 10cm (4 inches) apart in rows 30cm (1 foot) apart (closer spacing gives smaller bulbs).

- Sow seeds for maincrop onions outside in March and April and thin plants to required spacing.

- Seeds for overwintering onions are sown from July to September.

- Spring or salad onions are grown from seed and can be sown successively from spring through to late summer.

- Onions need to be kept well weeded.

Harvest

- Onions are mature once their tops fall over naturally.

- They are lifted and left on the soil to dry (in fair weather) or are dried inside if necessary.

- Once the skins are papery dry they can be plaited for storage.

- Maincrop onions are ready for harvest in July and August.

- Overwintered onions are ready in June.

- Maincrop onions are better for long-term storage.

- Spring onions are harvested as they reach an acceptable size.

Problems

- Onions are susceptible to several diseases. The worst, white rot, can live in the soil for years.

- Buy your sets from reputable sources and maintain good hygiene on your plot to avoid it.

PARSNIPS

- The humble parsnip is a winter staple and part of the traditional English roast dinner.

- Parsnips belong to the same vegetable family as carrots and parsley.

- Unlike carrots, parsnips are not considered to be a good container crop. Grow in the ground, on a large plot or allotment.

Pocket Fact

In rare cases the sap in parsnip foliage can cause phytophotodermatitis: 'burns' on skin exposed to sap and sunlight.

Grow

- Parsnip seed does not store well – you'll need to buy fresh seeds every year.

- Seeds are sown from February through to the end of May, in rows 30cm (1 foot) apart.

- Parsnip seed is slow to germinate and is often sown with radishes which germinate quickly and mark the row.

- The radishes are harvested before the parsnips need space.

- Thin seedlings to 15cm (6 inches) apart.

- Like carrots, parsnips like loose and well-drained soil and will fork if they are overfed.

Harvest

- The harvest begins after the first frosts, and roots can be left in the ground until March.

- You can also use a closer spacing and harvest some plants young for baby roots.

Problems

- Seeds may fail to germinate in cold soil; later sowings tend to be more successful.

- Uneven watering causes roots to split, so try to keep the soil evenly wet.

PEAS

- There's nothing quite like the taste of home-grown peas, fresh from the pod.

- Peas (like beans) are legumes and can form relationships with nitrogen-fixing bacteria in the soil.

- The choice of dwarf or climbing varieties means peas can find a home on most plots.

Pocket Fact ✎

Pea seeds are said to have been unearthed from the tombs of the Pharaohs.

Grow

- Pea seeds are either 'round' or 'wrinkled'. The round-seeded varieties are slightly more hardy and can be sown in autumn for early spring harvests. Both types can be sown in spring (March to June).

- Traditional pea varieties are tall and need substantial supports (like runner beans). Modern varieties are much shorter and only need 'pea sticks', which are short, twiggy sticks.

- Keep plants well watered, but don't overfeed.

Harvest

- Harvest the pods as soon as the peas start to swell.

- Picking the pods encourages more to form.

- Autumn-sown peas crop in May; spring-sown plants crop from July to October.

- Peas are at their sweetest straight out of the pod, so only pick those you want to eat immediately.

- Mangetout varieties are harvested when the pods are young, before the peas start to swell.

- You can also harvest 'peashoots' from your plants, which are the tender-top leaves and tendrils; the plant will bush out and grow more.

- Throughout the year you can also sow pea seeds close together in shallow trays of compost to harvest peashoots as a salad vegetable.

Problems

- Pea moth larvae damage crops from May through to the end of July. Early and late sowings usually avoid damage.

- Mice love pea seeds and can eat entire rows before they germinate. Try sowing in a length of guttering (held off the ground) and sliding the entire length into a shallow trench once the seedlings are growing strongly.

- Slugs and snails also love pea seedlings.

PEPPERS

- Sweet and chilli peppers are recent additions to the allotment crop list. They love sunshine, and come in an amazing array of shapes and sizes.

- Peppers respond well to being grown in containers, and love windowsills.

Pocket Fact

The Scoville scale is a measure of the heat of chilli peppers. Sweet peppers score 0; the ghost chilli scores over 1,000,000.

Grow

- Pepper seeds are sown indoors in February and March.

- They need warmth to germinate, but room temperature is usually warm enough.

- Pot on seedlings as necessary and plant out after the risk of frost has passed.

- Keep plants well watered and give a high potash (tomato) feed once they begin to flower.

- They love sunshine, and a sunny spot is important. They also grow well under cover.

Harvest
- Peppers can be harvested at any stage.

- They usually begin to form in one colour and ripen to a different one.

Problems
- It can be hard to ripen peppers in short British summers. Choose an early variety or smaller peppers.

- Chillies can be easier, but the heat is dependent on the climate as well as the variety.

POTATOES
- A tuber crop that needs no introduction, potatoes are an integral part of most vegetable plots.

- Always buy seed potatoes rather than saving your own or planting supermarket potatoes, as they are guaranteed disease-free.

- Maincrop potatoes take a lot of space and are best grown on allotments and large plots.

- Smaller plots can afford a bed of earlies, and they also provide reasonable harvests in large containers if kept well watered.

Pocket Fact

Potatoes belong to the same plant family as deadly nightshade, and this relationship caused them to be met with suspicion when they were first brought to Europe from the New World.

Grow

- Seed potatoes are available from February, and are traditionally planted outside on Good Friday.

- In between, they're 'chitted' – left on a cool windowsill to sprout in the light. Good 'chits' are short and green; left in the dark they are spindly and pale.

- There are many different types of potatoes, each with slightly different planting and harvest times.

- If you want to store potatoes through the winter, you want maincrop varieties.

- Most people can't resist 'first earlies' (new potatoes) and salad potatoes are also early, and popular.

- Plant earlies 10cm (4 inches) deep and others 20cm (8 inches) deep, 30cm (1 foot) apart.

- As soon as the leaves start to emerge you 'earth them up' – literally bury them under a mound of soil (or you can use a thick layer of mulch). Keep doing this until the potato plant is growing out of a big mound. Earthing up makes potatoes more productive, and helps prevent tubers from growing green when exposed to light.

Harvest

- Early potatoes are ready once they begin to flower. Harvest them as you want them, as they're best fresh.

- Each variety has an ideal harvest time, so check the label.

- Maincrop potatoes are lifted at the end of the season and spread on the ground for a couple of days to set the skins before storage.

- Dig over your potato bed thoroughly, to avoid missing tubers that will sprout again next year. This can ruin your rotation.

Problems

- Blight attacks in humid weather (usually late summer) and cuts foliage down in days. Once you spot it, cut down the foliage and throw it away. Leave the potatoes underground for a couple of weeks to protect them from the blight spores. They are unlikely to store well, so eat them fresh.

- Scab is a problem on alkaline soils (high pH values) but the damage is largely cosmetic.

RADISHES

- Punchy, crunchy and quick-to-grow, radishes are a vegetable plot favourite.

- Winter radishes are grown in the soil, but small summer radishes are perfect for small plots and containers.

Pocket Fact 🗝
Ten radishes counts as one of your five-a-day.

Grow

- Sow radishes direct in small batches from February right through to September.

- Keep the plants well watered and weed-free.

- Winter radishes (mooli and daikon) are sown from midsummer through to September.

Harvest

- Pull roots as they become large enough and before they become too old and tough.

- Winter radishes are best left in the soil until you want them, from October through to December.

Problems

- Flea beetles eat holes in the leaves.

- As brassicas, radishes can also be affected by club root.

RUNNER BEANS

- As members of the legume family, runner beans are allotment and kitchen garden favourites.
- They are tall, heavy cropping plants that require a sturdy support.
- The red flowers are very pretty.
- The dwarf variety 'Hestia' is suitable for growing in containers and on small plots.
- There are also 'stringless' cultivars bred to have more tender pods.

Grow

- Runner beans like soil to which plenty of compost has been added.
- Sow seeds indoors in April for planting outside in May (or once the risk of frost has passed) or sow outside, where they are to grow, in May and June.
- Sow seeds in pairs, and space 30cm (1 foot) apart. They are often grown in double rows, 60cm (2 feet) apart.
- Plants climb from a young age, so make the support before you plant them out.

Harvest

- Runner beans are prolific, cropping from July through to the first frosts of autumn.
- Keep picking beans as they reach a suitable size; constant harvesting encourages more pods to form.

Problems

- In hot weather the flowers can fail to 'set', and drop off without forming pods. Give the plants plenty of water, and mist the foliage as well to encourage a good set.

- As with other bean seeds, mice may eat them before they germinate. Sow in pots if this is a problem.

- Slugs may bother seedlings, and mature plants can be attacked by blackfly.

Pocket Fact 🪏

Usually grown as an annual in the UK, runner beans are tender perennials. It is possible to lift the roots in autumn and store them (like dahlias) in trays of damp sand or compost, somewhere frost-free. They can then be replanted in May to grow again.

SWEETCORN

- This is another crop that's far nicer home-grown and eaten within minutes of being harvested.

- Modern 'super-sweet' varieties are very popular.

- Sweetcorn is best in the ground, on a large plot. You need a big enough block of plants to ensure good pollination.

Pocket Fact 🪏

Sweetcorn is pollinated by the wind, which is why it's grown in blocks.

Grow

- Sow seeds in April inside for planting out in May, or sow outside in May.

- Plants need to be 30cm (1 foot) apart in a block, not rows.

- Keep well watered and fed.

Harvest

- Cobs are ready when the silky strands at the end turn brown. Peel back the husk and nick a nugget with your fingernail – if it's milky then the corn is ready.

- Harvest only what you need, and cook as quickly as possible, as it's sweetest fresh.

- Baby sweetcorn varieties are harvested when the cobs are very small.

Problems

- On windy sites plants may be rocked by the wind as they get taller; give them some support as they're growing.

- Poor pollination causes patchy cobs. Remember to plant sweetcorn in a block.

- 'Supersweet' varieties have to be kept separate from other varieties to avoid cross-pollination and a resulting lack of sweetness. In a garden or allotment setting it's easier to separate them by time (two to three weeks) than by distance, so stagger your seed sowing.

TOMATOES

- An indispensable part of the British summer, tomatoes are easy to grow.

- Technically a fruit (like peppers and aubergines), tomatoes are usually eaten as a vegetable.

- There's a tomato to fit in every spot. Cherry tomatoes are the quickest and easiest to grow.

Pocket Fact ⚊

Like its relative the potato, the tomato was greeted with suspicion when it first arrived in Europe.

Grow

- Seeds are sown indoors in February, to be planted out after the risk of frost.

- There are greenhouse and outdoor varieties.

- Indeterminate plants are tall and sprawling – they need training. You also have to remove side shoots as they appear, as tomatoes struggle to ripen fruit in the British climate.

- Determinate (or bush) plants are smaller and need no pruning.

- Tomatoes need to be kept well watered. Give a regular tomato feed once the plants start flowering.

Harvest

- Harvest fruit as they ripen to red (although some are harvested yellow).

- Any green fruits remaining at the end of the season can be cooked or used for chutney.

PROBLEMS

- Blight (as for potatoes; see p.105) can destroy the plants very quickly.

- Blossom end rot is caused by uneven watering.

♛ HERBS ♛

Most herbs are happy in containers and fit on to the smallest plot. All herbs are at their best when regularly harvested – keep them close and pick a bunch as you need it.

BASIL

- Basil leaves are perfect for pasta sauces, pizza and tomato salads.

- Sweet basil is the classic variety.

- You could also try bush basil (small leaves) and lettuce-leaved basil (big leaves). Other varieties have different flavours.

Pocket Tip 🖙

You can turn basil into pesto and freeze it for winter use, but don't add the parmesan cheese before freezing.

Grow

- Basil is an annual herb.

- Sow seeds inside in spring.

- Basil loves rich soil, plenty of water and sunshine. It can grow on a sunny windowsill in winter.

CHIVES

- Snipped chives add an onion flavour to many dishes, including the humble baked potato.

- Chive flowers are also edible.

Pocket Fact 🖙

Garlic chives have flatter leaves, a garlicky flavour and white flowers.

Grow

- Chives are a perennial herb.

- Sow seeds inside in spring.

- Easy-to-care for and hardy through the winter.

- Both flowers and leaves are edible.

MINT

- Add to salads or new potatoes, or refreshing summer drinks and dips.

- Peppermint and spearmint plants are widely available.

- Other flavours are available, but they're often less hardy.

Pocket Tip 🛒

Grow different varieties of mint separately as the flavours tend to mingle.

Grow

- Mint is a perennial herb.

- Buy a small plant in spring and plant out or pot up.

- Mint can be invasive and is often planted in pots that are sunk into the ground to keep it contained.

- It needs repotting or dividing in spring.

- Mint in containers needs plenty of water in summer.

- Bring a pot inside for winter use.

PARSLEY

- Often overlooked, parsley is green through the worst weather and packed with vitamins and minerals.

- Add it to salads and stir-fries or make a classic parsley sauce.

- Flat-leaved and curly parsley are both widely available as seed or young plants.

Pocket Tip 🛒

Try briefly deep-frying curly parsley to make a crispy garnish.

Grow

- Parsley is a biennial herb.

- Sow the seeds inside in spring – it can take several weeks to sprout, but warm conditions help.

- A second sowing in late summer will give you parsley through until spring.

- Parsley flowers attract beneficial insects to your plot.

ROSEMARY

- This is a lovely addition to roast lamb or garlic bread.
- Many varieties are available, divided into two main types: prostrate (low-growing) and upright.

Pocket Tip

Toss rosemary stems onto the barbecue to add a fragrant note.

Grow

- Rosemary is a perennial herb.
- Buy a young plant in spring and plant out or pot on.
- It likes a sunny spot and well-drained soil, but containers need watering in dry weather.

THYME

- Thyme is good with meat dishes, especially slow-cooked stews and soups.
- Many varieties are available, with different growing habits and flavours.

Grow

- Thyme is a perennial herb, which grows in the same way as rosemary.

Pocket Fact

Together with parsley and bay, thyme forms the basis of a bouquet garni.

☙ SOFT FRUIT ❧

Soft fruit is the easiest type to start with, and can fit into any plot.

BLACKBERRIES

- It's fun to forage for brambles, but quicker to grow your own.

- Choose a thornless variety in smaller gardens, to avoid being scratched.

Pocket Fact 🔨

Blackberries aren't fruits. Like raspberries, they are aggregate fruits composed of single-seeded drupes.

Grow

- Blackberries and hybrid berries (including tayberries and loganberries) are easy to grow.

- They don't take up much space if trained on to a wall or fence.

- They love rich, moisture-retentive soil and are most productive in a sunny spot.

- You only need one plant, as they are self-fertile, but they're too vigorous to grow well in containers.

- Prune out year-old canes once they have fruited.

BLACKCURRANTS

- Blackcurrants can be cooked into pies and jams or used to make cordial.

- Blackcurrants are very rich in vitamin C, making them another home-grown superfruit.

Grow

- Blackcurrants like a rich, well-drained soil.

- They're hardy, but avoid planting them in frost pockets for the best results.

- Plant out 6cm ($2\frac{1}{2}$ inches) deeper than plants were in their pots, to encourage good growth.

- Prune all the stems to a few inches during the first winter.

- Give plants a nitrogen-rich fertiliser (or a layer of compost) in spring, and plenty of water in summer.

- After the first few years, prune out the oldest canes in winter.

- Container-grown plants need repotting every two to three years. Trim roots and replace the top layer of compost with fresh if replanting in the same pot.

- A net may be needed to protect fruit from birds.

BLUEBERRIES

- An American classic, blueberries have been touted as a superfruit.

- If you only have space for one bush, make sure it's a self-fertile variety.

Pocket Tip

Try underplanting your blueberries with cranberries — they're low-growing and love acidic soil.

Grow

- Blueberries need acidic soil (a low pH); if you don't have it they have to be grown in containers.

- Collect rainwater to keep the plants well watered.

- Pruning is limited to removing dead wood.

- Birds love eating blueberries, so net plants if they are a problem.

RASPBERRIES

- Although a classic summer fruit, raspberry varieties are divided into summer- and autumn-fruiting.

- If you have a large plot, grow both types to extend the season.
- Raspberries are also available with yellow fruits.

Pocket Fact 🌱

Most of the raspberries sold in the UK are grown in Scotland.

Grow

- Raspberry canes are usually bought as bare-root plants in winter, and planted while dormant.
- Space plants 30cm (1 foot) apart in rich soil.
- Summer raspberries need sturdy supports; use autumn raspberries in containers.
- Prune summer raspberry canes to the ground when they finish fruiting and tie the new canes into the support.
- Prune autumn raspberry canes in midwinter.
- Birds are as fond of raspberries as we are! You may need to net your bushes, or grow them in a fruit cage, to protect the harvest.

RHUBARB

- Botanically a vegetable, rhubarb is eaten as a fruit early in the year when little is available.
- A rhubarb plant makes good use of a problem corner in a small garden, but it is not productive in containers.

Pocket Fact 🌱

The 'Rhubarb Triangle' in West Yorkshire grows large crops of forced rhubarb in special forcing sheds.

Grow

- Rhubarb can be grown from seed but it's usually bought as a plant or a one-year-old 'crown'.

- Plant spacing is 90cm (3 feet).

- Rhubarb loves rich soil and copes with partial shade.

- Stems are harvested in May and June. Twist from the base, then pull.

- The leaves are poisonous, but are safe to compost.

- You can 'force' a mature plant to produce an earlier harvest of sweeter (and paler) stems, by covering it with a bucket before the new leaves start to emerge. Remove the bucket once the harvest is finished.

STRAWBERRIES

- An easy fruit crop that fits into even the tiniest of plots.

- Grow more than one variety to extend the season.

- Alpine strawberries grow tiny fruits all through the summer, and are grown from seed.

Pocket Tip

Try sprinkling your strawberries with black pepper for a new taste sensation.

Grow

- Buy small plants in spring and plant out or pot on.

- The plants like plenty of water and a sunny spot.

- Use straw to keep the fruits off the ground and clean, or grow in containers.

- Strawberry plants grow 'runners' during the summer – long stems with plantlets at the end. Pot up the plantlets to make new plants (don't cut the runner until the new plant is growing roots).

- Strawberry plants are best replaced every three years.

♛ EDIBLE FLOWERS ♛

Edible flowers are an easy way to make your plot beautiful and productive. If you're not familiar with these plants, make sure you've correctly identified them before tucking in.

BORAGE

- Borage (*Borago officinalis*) is an annual.

- Borage flowers are a pretty blue colour (a white variety is also available) and popular with beneficial insects.

- They appear from June to November and have a light cucumber flavour.

- Add to salads and summer drinks or freeze into ice cubes for a summery effect.

Pocket Fact ⚲

Although now widely grown, borage originally comes from Syria.

Grow

- Sow seeds in spring and plant out 30cm (1 foot) apart.

- Borage is trouble-free and unfussy about soil and location.

- It is happy in containers, but grows larger, up to 90cm (3 feet) tall, in the ground.

- Taller plants can suffer from wind damage.

- If you leave some flowers for the bees, borage happily self-seeds, meaning you only have to sow it once to have it every year.

- Unwanted plants are easily weeded out.

CALENDULA

- Calendula (*Calendula officinalis*) is an annual.

- It is the pot marigold (not to be confused with French and African marigolds) – a lovely orange daisy-like flower that is much loved by bees and beneficial insects.

- The petals are used in place of saffron, or to add colour to salads.

Pocket Fact 🍵

Calendula is also used in herbal medicine.

Grow

- Sow seeds in spring.

- Calendula is unfussy about site and soil, but will flower more readily in a sunny spot.

- Flowers appear from June to November, and plants self-seed if seed heads are not removed.

DANDELIONS

- A lovely flower that is almost effortless to grow, as it is a common 'weed'.

- Flowers can be added to fritters, or used to make herbal tea and wine.

Pocket Tip 🛒

You can force dandelion plants by covering them with a bucket, for a crop of tender salad leaves early in the year.

Grow

- Dandelion is a perennial.

- Dandelion (*Taraxacum officinale*) seeds are available if you don't have any in your garden.

- Seeds are sown in spring, and should be potted on into deep pots as the plants have long roots.

- Dandelions self-seed very readily if the flowers are not removed.

NASTURTIUMS

- With their open flowers and sunny colours, nasturtiums add a splash of colour to the garden.

- Both the flowers and leaves are edible, with a peppery flavour. They can be added to salads.

Pocket Tip 🛒

Nasturtium seeds can be pickled and used like capers.

Grow

- Nasturtium is an annual.

- Nasturtiums (*Tropaeolum majus*) are easily grown from their large seeds, and will self-seed if allowed.

- For good flower production they need poor soil; overfeeding causes leaves to grow at the expense of flowers.

- Nasturtiums are good for attracting beneficial insects.

- They also act as a 'trap crop' – attracting blackfly and cabbage butterflies away from other plants, so they can be controlled, or the plants destroyed.

- Nasturtiums are killed by frost, but readily self-seed.

SAFFRON

- Saffron is the most expensive spice in the world, because it has to be picked by hand.

- It come from the saffron crocus (*Crocus sativus*). Other crocuses are poisonous, and should not be eaten.

Pocket Fact ⬢

In the 16th and 17th centuries, saffron was widely grown around the British town now known as Saffron Walden.

Grow

- Saffron is a perennial.
- Saffron is grown from corms – source yours from a reputable supplier.
- It originates from the Mediterranean and has an unusual growth pattern. Saffron is dormant in the dry summer months (when the corms are planted) and comes back into growth in the wetter days of autumn.
- Purple flowers develop in October and November, and the spice itself comprises the three red stigmas inside the flower. These are harvested as soon as the flowers open, then dried inside for future use.
- Your saffron harvest won't make you rich, but considering the retail price it makes a worthwhile addition to a flower bed or container.
- Plant corms 10cm (4 inches) deep. The corms multiply over time and should be lifted in the summer every four years and replanted separately.

VIOLA

- The sweet violet (*Viola odorata*) is a small purple flower with a sweet scent.
- Heartsease (*Viola tricolor*) varieties have the familiar pansy 'faces', on a smaller scale, and are available in many colour combinations.

Pocket Fact ⬢

Most violas have heart-shaped leaves, and flowers that are not symmetrical.

Grow

- Violas are very hardy plants.

- The sweet violet likes some shade, and happily grows underneath other plants.

- The flowers are usually candied and used as cake decorations.

- Heartsease makes more of a show, and brightens up containers.

- Flowers are available for much of the year and can be added to salads.

- Plants will self-seed if flowers are not removed.

♛ OTHER PLOT RESIDENTS: ♛ WILDLIFE

Depending on the location and size of your plot you will probably find that vegetables and herbs are not the only residents on your plot. People often find that the wildlife they encounter on their plot can be as enjoyable as growing their own produce. However, there are some animals you don't want to encourage on to an allotment. Pigeons love eating brassicas, badgers love sweetcorn, and deer and rabbits eat anything. Even foxes can be problematic as they tend to dig up things fertilised with bone meal. Rats and mice are not popular visitors either.

Having said that, a wildlife-friendly plot will benefit from pest control from birds, hedgehogs and slow worms. A healthier ecosystem leads to healthier plants, and fewer pest problems overall.

TYPES OF WILDLIFE YOU CAN EXPECT

Before you begin to attract wildlife, you have to stop poisoning it. Adding chemicals (fertilisers, pesticides and herbicides) to your soil breaks the food web right at the bottom. Slug pellets regularly poison hedgehogs, and if there are no pests to eat, you won't attract any beneficial insects. Bees are particularly susceptible to insecticides.

Flowers will attract bees, hoverflies and butterflies. Ladybirds look for aphid populations in which to lay their eggs – leave a few nettles at the edge of the plot for them. Don't keep everything too tidy, as many creatures feed on or live in decaying organic matter. They also need debris in which to overwinter. Most commercial wildlife habitats are unnecessary if you leave a corner of the patch to grow wild.

Make compost and use it to feed the soil. It encourages the organisms at the bottom of the food web, which means food for the animals higher up.

BEES

There are many species of bee in the UK, including honey bees, bumblebees and solitary bees. They all feed on nectar and pollen from flowers, so attracting them is a matter of growing a variety of flowers all through the year.

Most vegetables either don't flower or are harvested before they do, but broad beans flower early in spring. Fruit blossom follows on (and strawberries flower over a long period). Many herbs also flower over a long period, and are good for bees. Rosemary, thyme, lavender and chives are all great.

Add in any edible flowers and flowers grown as companion plants, and an allotment can be a paradise for bees. They even benefit from the flowers on green manures – phacelia and clover are particularly valuable.

Keeping bees

Many plots do not allow beehives, but some do, and you could have a hive in a back garden. You need to think carefully, though, as your neighbours may worry about being stung (especially if they have children). Bees need regular care throughout spring and summer, and occasional care though autumn and winter.

Start-up costs can be considerable, as you'll need a hive and a protective suit. Bees themselves are usually sourced from swarms (existing colonies split to form new ones) captured by beekeepers.

Before committing to bees, contact your local beekeeping association. They all run training courses for beginners, to show you how to care for your bees and process the honey.

CHICKENS

Some allotment sites welcome livestock with open arms, but on others they are completely forbidden. Once you have established that you can keep chickens, you'll need to consider very carefully whether you should. A constant supply of eggs may sound tempting, but chickens need daily attention. If you're friendly with a neighbouring plotholder then consider combining efforts, so that you can share the rewards and burdens of caring for your birds.

Sourcing hens

Source your chickens from a reputable local breeder. Go and see the conditions they're kept in, and make sure you ask whether they've had their vaccinations. Hens are usually supplied as 'point of lay' – old enough to take care of themselves and to lay eggs.

Care

Hens need the following:

- **Shelter**. A waterproof coop is essential.
- **Fencing**. To keep your chickens from destroying your crops and to keep predators out.
- **Food**. Laying hens produce an egg every day, but only with a decent diet. Layers pellets or mash are their staple food, but eggs are tastier if hens have access to fresh greens or grass.
- **Grit**. Laying hens need grit for digestion and extra calcium (to form eggshells), normally supplied as crushed oyster shell.
- **Water**. A constant supply of clean water is required.
- **Medical attention**. Check that there is a local vet with chicken experience if you live in an urban area.

Chickens love eating pests – including slugs, snails, earwigs, ants and ant eggs. They keep down the grass, peck at the weeds, scratch over the soil and leave little parcels of fertility everywhere they go.

Left unsupervised though, they eat their favourite vegetables down to the ground, scratch up seedlings and use your seedbed as a dustbath. They eat the lower leaves off any tasty trees and bushes, and snaffle any soft fruit within their reach.

But hens come running when they see you, and greet you with friendly squawks and cheeps. The sight of a chicken sunbathing, or enjoying a good bath in the dirt, is a worthwhile addition to the allotment experience.

Pocket Tip

It's illegal to carry food waste from your home to your allotment, either to compost it or to feed it to your chickens. It's fine to give them crops from the allotment itself though.

8

STORING YOUR PRODUCE AND SEEDS

Although one of the joys of having an allotment is the fresh, seasonal food that it produces, there will be times when you have a surplus. You can share it with friends, swap it for something different, or store it for later use. In this chapter we look at ways in which you can store your crops, and also how to look after your seeds to keep them fresh for next year.

HARVESTING TO STORE

> ### *Handy hints for harvesting your crops to help them to last longer in storage*
>
> - *Pick crops at their peak. Fruits and vegetables that are past their best won't store as well.*
> - *Over-ripe vegetables and fruits can be used for preserves or cooked dishes.*
> - *Examine produce carefully for any signs of pest damage or disease. Use any that aren't perfect now, and save the best for storage.*
> - *Leafy vegetables and herbs are at their peak in the morning.*
> - *If you're picking vegetables and herbs to dry, wait for the morning dew to evaporate before you harvest.*

STORING PRODUCE

If you're going to store crops then they need to be at their best, and fresh, so it's important to store them at the right time of the year.

WHAT'S IN SEASON?

Spring

The tender new shoots of spring are often long awaited and in short supply, so gluts at this time of year are uncommon. However, the season for some vegetables is so short that you may want to store some of your harvest for later. See p.129 for more information about storage methods.

Vegetables ready for harvest in spring include asparagus, broad beans, purple sprouting broccoli and leafy vegetables such as kale, cabbage, spinach and chard. There should also be fresh growth on herbs such as chives and parsley that have been in the ground all winter. For fruit, there's rhubarb.

Summer

Summer is the season of plenty. Although the first new potatoes and ripe tomatoes are eagerly savoured, it's easy to become tired of their flavours later on. Storing your surplus now allows you to bring a taste of summer to the winter months.

Summer vegetables include aubergines, calabrese, cucumbers, French and runner beans, peas, peppers and tomatoes, and salads. Many herbs are at their best in summer, particularly basil, and the soft-fruit harvest arrives in this season too.

Autumn

As the temperature drops and the days get shorter it's time to gather in anything that is harmed by winter weather. In most of the UK the first frosts of autumn will arrive in October, so aim to harvest and store these crops before the end of September.

Vegetables to harvest now include beetroot and carrots, marrows and squashes, garlic and onions. It's also the time to lift potatoes and to pick apples and pears.

Winter

In the cold months of winter there's not much in active growth, but you'll be harvesting hardy vegetables such as celeriac,

Jerusalem artichokes, kale, leeks, Brussels sprouts and parsnips. There are salad vegetables that survive the cooler months, but the fruit harvests are over and most herbs are off the menu. This is when your stored crops are most useful.

♛ STORAGE METHODS ♛

REFRIGERATION

It's easy enough to pop fruit and vegetables into the fridge for a few days, and it's a great method for short-term storage. But how do you make sure that your produce is still fresh when you come to use it?

For most vegetables and fruits, the key is not to wash them before you put them in the fridge. Although they may be a bit dirty, too much moisture encourages them to rot. Pop them straight in the fridge, and wash them when you want to use them. This is particularly true for soft fruit, which is very fragile.

However, you can keep salad leaves fresh for a few days by washing them (and not drying them thoroughly) and storing them in the fridge in a plastic bag or airtight container. A small amount of water helps stop them wilting; the same is true for sprouting broccoli heads.

If you have a bunch of celery or leafy herbs, then pop them in a glass of water in the fridge to keep them at their best.

Pocket Tip 🐖
Refrigeration is only for short-term storage. Don't let your vegetables languish for too long!

Works best for . . .

- Spring vegetables such as asparagus and purple sprouting broccoli.
- Leafy vegetables such as cabbage and chard.

- Salads.

- Soft fruit.

FREEZING

A freezer is another indispensable appliance in modern homes, and freezing vegetables and fruits is a useful way of storing them for future use. There are two points you need to bear in mind.

- Fruits and vegetables aren't the same once they are frozen. There may be changes in texture and/or flavour.

- Your harvest is at risk from any loss of power that lasts for more than a couple of hours, and you could lose the lot if your freezer breaks down.

Pocket Tip

The key to successful long-term storage is not to put all your eggs in one basket — don't put everything in the freezer.

Many foods are best cooked into dishes before being frozen. For example, making and freezing large batches of pasta sauce is a great way to store tomatoes, aubergine, onions and peppers.

Other vegetables need to be blanched (boiled briefly) to preserve their flavour and colour.

Don't freeze more of each vegetable than you're likely to use before it comes back into season — eating your produce fresh is the big joy of growing your own.

Works best for . . .

- Aubergines and tomatoes — cook into sauces and finished dishes.

- Broad beans, green beans and peas — blanch before freezing.

- Onions and peppers — chop up and open-freeze on trays before bagging up.

- Sweetcorn – blanch and remove kernels from the cob.

- Leafy herbs – chop and freeze into ice cubes.

BOTTLING, CANNING AND PRESERVES

Bottling (canning in the USA) involves preserving fruits and vegetables in tightly sealed jars. Most foods have to be thoroughly cooked, and many need the addition of vinegar to ensure that bacteria doesn't grow in the bottles during storage. You also need to make sure that everything used in the bottling process is sterilised before use.

If you want to store your produce this way, you'll need to find more information; there are numerous ways to poison yourself if you're not careful! The Allotment Growing website (http://allotment.org.uk) is a good place to start your research, and Fruit Expert (www.fruitexpert.co.uk) has information on storing and preserving fruit.

Pocket Tip 🌾

Our understanding of food safety has improved by leaps and bounds in the past few decades, so look for modern information about safe bottling rather than relying on age-old wisdom.

Preserves

One of the most popular ways of storing a glut is to transform it into preserves – jams, marmalades, chutneys and pickles are endlessly useful to add colour and flavour to winter meals, and also make great homemade gifts.

If you follow a recipe it takes care of all the food safety issues, and should let you know how long your chosen preserve keeps. A list of the equipment you're likely to need is given on p.136.

Pocket Tip

Start saving jam jars and lids now. You can wash and sterilise them properly once you're ready to use them.

Works best for . . .

- Pickled onions and beetroot.

- Soft-fruit jams and cordials – strawberry, raspberry and blackberry.

- Tree fruit in syrups – plums and apples

- Savoury chutneys – onions, marrows, green tomatoes.

DRYING

Drying has passed out of favour for vegetables, now that we have fridges and freezers, but is still used a lot for storing herbs.

How to dry herbs

1. Pick fresh herbs through the growing season, but before the plants flower.
2. Harvest leaves in dry weather, before the sun gets too hot, for the best flavour.
3. Separate the leaves so that they dry more quickly.
4. Lay them out on clean paper on top of a wire rack, so there's good air flow.
5. Put the rack somewhere warm and dark, but with air movement (so not the airing cupboard!).
6. Turn leaves every day, so that they dry evenly.
7. Leaves are ready to be stored in jars or tins once they're completely dry and crumbly.

Drying is often used in Asia, where pak choi leaves are air-dried and used for winter soups. In sunnier climates drying is used to preserve grapes (as raisins and sultanas) and sun-dried tomatoes.

Beans also lend themselves to being stored dried, although they then have to be thoroughly cooked – a pressure cooker comes in handy to cut down on the cooking time. Beans are best left to dry thoroughly on the plants, until the pods are brown and crispy. If bad weather threatens, uproot the plants and hang them upside down in the shed to finish drying.

Works best for . . .

- Mediterranean herbs: rosemary, thyme, lavender.

- Tomatoes, apple slices (in a dehydrator, or on a low heat in the oven).

- Chillies (small fruit with thin skins dry most easily).

COLD STORAGE

Root vegetables tend to be best stored in cool conditions. The traditional method for storing roots such as carrots and beetroot is to build a clamp in autumn. The vegetables are dug up, the worst of the soil is brushed off them (and the leaves are twisted off), and then the roots are stacked into a pile on a bed of dry straw. The pile is covered in a thick layer of straw, about 20cm (8 inches) deep, and then buried in a layer of soil. The clamp keeps roots cool and moist, prevents frost damage and allows you to access your crop even when the ground itself is frozen solid.

If you have a shed or garage then a slightly different technique involves storing your crop in trays of damp sand or potting compost.

1. Put a centimetre or so of damp sand or potting compost into the bottom of a tray or box.

2. Carefully place each root in the tray so that they don't touch.

3. Cover with more damp sand or compost.

4. Add more layers as necessary.

5. Don't overcrowd your trays, and keep them off the ground and away from mice.

Apples and pears can also be stored in trays, but each fruit is wrapped in paper so that they do not touch, and no sand is added. Potatoes can be stored in paper or hessian sacks that exclude light but allow them to breathe.

Pocket Tip 🐄

The key to cold storage is to regularly check your stores and remove any items that are starting to rot or look past their best.

Works best for . . .

● Root vegetables: potatoes, carrots, parsnips and beetroot.

● Apples and pears.

ROOM TEMPERATURE STORAGE

Some vegetables are actually happiest when stored at room temperature – kept from freezing temperatures, but not too warm.

Winter squashes

To store squashes, cut them fully ripe with a T-shaped section of stem, which helps prevents rot from setting in at the top of the fruit. Don't use it as a handle; it won't support the weight. Leave them on a warm windowsill for a couple of weeks until the skin has cured nice and hard in the sun.

Different varieties of squash store for different lengths of time – check the seed packet to see how long yours will last. Most will store through to Christmas and into the New Year. Try cutting your stored squashes into wedges for roasting, or cut into chunks for soup.

Onions and garlic

Onions and garlic are traditionally plaited into strings and hung in the kitchen or pantry. Lift your onions and garlic once their tops have started to go yellow and flop over. Ideally they're left on the ground in the sun for a few days to 'cure', but the UK climate tends to be too damp for this to work. If the weather is wet then lay them out on trays inside and wait for the skins to dry until they are papery.

Any onions that have a thick neck won't store, so separate those out to use now. You can store your garlic and onion bulbs by hanging them in nets (after removing the stems), or you can use the dried stems to plait them into strings.

How to plait onions and garlic

1. Trim stems to 10cm (4 inches).
2. Cut a length of string around 1.5m (5 feet) long (the length depends on how many onions you have to store, but it's best not to hang too many together).
3. Fold the string in half and knot the loose ends together, so you have a loop.
4. Hang your loop from the back of a chair or something at a comfortable working height.
5. Twist the bottom of the loop to form a small loop and then place this around the neck of the first onion. Tighten it up until the onion is held in place.
6. Hold the second onion with the stem in one hand and the bulb in the other. Put the stem behind both lengths of string, then weave the bulb between the strings one way, then back the other way, so the stem forms an S or Z shape.
7. Do the same with the third onion, but from the other side.
8. Keep adding onions – each onion locks the previous one into position.
9. When the plait gets too large or heavy, start another. Simply knot any excess string to tie off the top, and hang your plait somewhere dry and airy (and not too hot).
10. You can trim any over-long stems to keep the plait neat.

EQUIPMENT FOR STORING

If you're using a fridge or a freezer then storing fruit and vegetables doesn't need anything other than common kitchen equipment such as saucepans and baking trays. For the more traditional storage techniques you'll need a little bit of equipment.

Preserving

A large saucepan or 'jam pan' allows you to make reasonable quantities. A preserving thermometer is essential, to ensure you cook food thoroughly and to know when jams reach their 'setting point'.

You'll also need clean jars with well-fitting lids. Depending on the preserve you may need plastic-lined lids (to prevent interaction with any acid contents). Some jams benefit from wax-paper layers before the lid goes on.

You'll need labels, so you know what you've made and when you made it, and for cordials and clear jellies you'll want some muslin cloths for straining.

Pocket Tip

It's possible to buy a special hand-operated passata machine that pulps tomatoes and removes all the seeds and skins for you in a jiffy.

Drying

Unfortunately Britain doesn't have the climate to produce sun-dried tomatoes in the back garden. You can get the same effect by drying them in the oven on the lowest possible setting all day, but if you want to dry other foods (or a lot of tomatoes) then it's probably worth investing in an electric dehydrator that does the job more efficiently.

♛ STORING SEEDS ♛

If you have a small plot then a commercial packet of seeds is likely to contain enough to fill your garden several times over.

Even if you have an entire allotment, you may not use all of a packet in one year.

You can club together with neighbours and friends to swap and share seeds, which cuts down on the cost, but inevitably you will want to store some seeds for next year. You may also want to start saving your own seeds from the plants in your garden.

STORING COMMERCIAL SEEDS

Storage tips

- Most seeds (including almost all common vegetables) keep best when they are kept cold, dry and in the dark.

- Keep seeds in a sealed box, to keep out moisture and mice.

- When you open a packet, keep seeds dry and re-seal the packet as thoroughly as you can.

- Keep a record of what you have, or use a filing system, so that you use up old seeds before buying fresh supplies.

- If you find packets of silica gel in things that you buy, save them and put them in your seed box.

- Don't leave your seed box in the greenhouse or anywhere subject to large changes in temperature.

Pocket Fact ✏

The Svalbard seed bank in the Arctic, and the Kew Millennium seed bank in West Sussex, keep seeds in very cold, dry conditions to store them for future generations.

SEED LIFESPANS

Commercial seed packets almost always come with a use-by date on them, which depends on the year in which they were packed. It's a useful guide to how long you can store your seeds, and when you may want to replace them, but they can be fairly generic.

In fact, different vegetable seeds survive for very different periods of time.

Average lifespan of seeds (years)	Vegetable
1	Parsnips (use fresh seed every year)
2	Beans, peas and parsley
3	Carrots, leeks, sweetcorn and tomatoes
4	Kale, lettuce and radish
5	Beetroot and chard, broccoli and cabbage
6	Marrows, courgettes and squashes
7	Cucumber

GERMINATION

Germination is the point at which dormant seeds (from a packet, or in the ground) start to come to life. They take in water, then send out a root. This is quickly followed by a shoot – the first visible sign of life.

Germination rates drop over time, so a packet of seeds that is past its use-by date may still give you plenty of plants if you sow more thickly than you usually would.

You can test your seed to see if it's still viable, and how well it will germinate. Simply dampen a sheet of kitchen roll, sprinkle a pinch of seeds on top, then fold up and place in a plastic bag or container. Keep your seeds at room temperature or somewhere warm (eg the airing cupboard) and check every day to see how many have germinated.

Pocket Tip 🛒

Sprouted seeds can be transplanted into compost to grow, if you're feeling frugal.

If germination rates are very low, or the seed rots before germinating, then it's time to buy fresh seed.

Larger seeds like peas and beans can be sprouted in jars. Soak the seeds in water overnight, then drain and rinse with clean water twice a day.

SAVING YOUR OWN SEED

There are many reasons why you might want to save your own seed. Perhaps you want to save money, or keep a favourite variety that's becoming hard to find. There are also heirloom and heritage seed varieties, and armies of amateur seed-savers who help to preserve them. And there's a surprising amount of politics involved in seed production and distribution; many people prefer to give as little money to seed companies as possible, or to avoid potential genetically modified contamination.

It's very easy to start saving your own seeds – just let a plant flower and set seed, and then collect it. But it's also a very complicated subject, and the more you know the better your results will be.

Top ten tips to saving your own seeds

1. *Annual seeds flower and set seed in one year, so they're a good place to start.*
2. *Biennial plants flower in their second year, so they may take up space for too long in a small garden.*
3. *For most plant seed, pods form as the flowers wilt, and are easily visible. They start green and dry to brown when the seeds are mature.*

4. *Saving your own seed is about getting the timing right — you want the seed to be mature, but you also want to collect the seed before it is dispersed.*

5. *Avoid plants that 'bolt' and flower too early; it may be a genetic trait you don't want to continue.*

6. *Some seeds are easier to clean and prepare for storage than others.*

7. *Many seedheads can be placed into paper bags, which catch the seeds as they ripen and fall from the stem.*

8. *Only save seeds from really ripe fruits (peppers, tomatoes, squashes, etc) as otherwise they won't be mature.*

9. *Store seeds in small paper envelopes (you can make your own) or splash out on re-sealable plastic bags for tiny seeds.*

10. *Remember to record the year you saved your seeds, as they don't live forever.*

INBREEDERS AND OUTBREEDERS

If a plant pollinates itself (is self-fertile) then the seeds it produces will grow into plants very much like their parent (they are said to come 'true'). In seed-saving terms, these plants are 'inbreeders', and they're easy to save seed from; you only need a few plants, and you don't have to worry about them cross-pollinating with other plants nearby. Inbreeders include peas and French beans, peppers and tomatoes.

'Outbreeders' are plants that cross-pollinate with others, which means that plants grown from seeds are likely to be very different from their parents. To save 'true' seeds from outbreeders you either need to erect barriers, or ensure a large distance between varieties. You also need to save seeds from a larger number of plants. Outbreeders include squashes and their relatives.

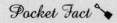

Pocket Fact

'Rogueing' is the process of removing plants and seeds that aren't true to type, so you avoid saving seeds that vary too much.

EASY SEEDS TO SAVE

Easy seeds to save for beginners include peas, French beans and peppers. They're all inbreeders, and if you grow only one variety at a time, you won't have any problems. The seeds are easily removed and dried for storage. Peas and beans are best left to dry on the plant (see p.133). For pepper seeds simply slice open a ripe fruit, remove the seeds and spread them out on a plate for a week or so to dry.

Tomatoes are also fairly easy, but the seeds need to be separated from the fleshy pulp. Try sticking them on to kitchen roll – you can cut the paper up and plant it with the seeds next year. Spinach and broad beans tend to cross-pollinate, but if you have a sheltered garden and only grow one variety, saving and cleaning the seed is easy.

If you develop the seed-saving bug, buy a book, or research on the internet, to find out how many plants you need for outbreeders, and the necessary spacing or protection needed to keep them 'true'.

SEASONAL GUIDE TO SEEDS

Spring

Very few fruits and vegetables flower and set seed in spring. One that does is purple sprouting broccoli, so if yours has gone to flower you could try saving your own seed. It's a difficult one, though, as it readily crosses with other varieties (so the resulting plants may be variable in terms of size, taste and other characteristics).

Chard, leaf beet and parsley planted last year run to seed in spring, and are easy to save seed from.

Summer

In summer you can save seeds from tomatoes, peppers and aubergines. Salad crops that run to seed are another opportunity, as are broad beans as they finish cropping.

Pocket Tip

Earmark a plant or two from which to save pea and bean seeds, as regular harvesting delays seed maturation and may mean you won't have any seeds ready to save at the end of the season.

Autumn

Autumn is when squashes ripen, and when you can save your own garlic bulbs for replanting. Sweetcorn is very difficult to save seed from because it crosses very easily, takes up a lot of space, and requires a long season for the seed to mature properly.

Pocket Tip

It's tempting to save potatoes, but they tend to harbour disease, so it's best to buy fresh seed potatoes every year.

Winter

There aren't many plants brave enough to flower and set seed in winter, but you can save some of your Jerusalem artichoke harvest to replant next year.

♛ PLANT PROPAGATION ♛

Growing from seed isn't the only way to increase your stock of plants. Vegetative propagation involves growing a new plant from a section of another. The technique used depends on the plant and the season.

SOFTWOOD CUTTINGS

Taken in spring or early summer, softwood cuttings are sections of fresh plant growth cut to just below a leaf. You end up with a length of stem with a leaf or two at the top; you don't want to leave too many leaves on. Push each cutting into fresh potting compost and keep moist with a fine mist of water until there are signs of new growth – then treat as seedlings.

Pocket Tip 🛒

The trick is to be quick with cuttings – the longer they are kept hanging around, the less likely they are to grow.

HARDWOOD CUTTINGS

Hardwood cuttings are taken in the same way as softwood cuttings, but in autumn from older stems. They take longer to grow new roots – perhaps several months.

Pocket Tip 🛒

Use a clean, sharp knife to take cuttings, to avoid disease problems.

LAYERING

Layering encourages a plant stem to grow roots by bringing it into contact with the soil. It's as simple as pegging a branch down, leaving it to form roots and then separating the new plant from its parent. You'll know when it has rooted because it has an obvious connection to the soil and a gentle tug won't budge it.

Pocket Fact 🔨

Blackberries and their relatives layer easily – they grow arching stems that root where they touch the ground.

DIVISION

Division involves taking a mature perennial plant and breaking it into smaller chunks, which are then replanted. It can be quite brutal – roots are tough – but it's a good way of splitting up mint plants or rejuvenating an old rhubarb crown. The traditional method uses two garden forks, back to back, to prize roots apart, but you can also use your secateurs to snip through.

Pocket Tip

Division is best done in spring or autumn.

9

PICKING AND EATING YOUR CROPS

Although gardening can be a pleasure in its own right, and it certainly has health benefits, there's not much point in having a kitchen garden if you don't eat what you grow. In this chapter we have a look at how you can fit home-grown produce into your meal plans, and some seasonal recipes to make the most of your crops.

♛ THE BENEFITS OF EATING ♛ SEASONALLY

- Eating seasonally means you have fresh flavours to look forward to every month.

- Food that is in season is fresh and better for you, and usually tastes better.

- Local, seasonal food is better for the environment than imported items.

- If you're buying your fruit and vegetables, they're cheaper when they're in season.

- Eating with the seasons helps you to reconnect with natural cycles.

Pocket Tip 🐛

The Eat Seasonably website (www.eatseasonably.co.uk) tells you which fruits and vegetables are in season each month, and offers recipes and serving suggestions. You can even download a colourful calendar to fix to the fridge.

♛ MEAL PLANNING ♛

When you're used to popping to the supermarket to buy all of your fruit and vegetables, harvesting and using your own can take a little getting used to.

Top ten tips to help you use your harvest

1. If you plan your meals in advance, visit your plot before you start and make a note of what's going to be ready to harvest this week – then plan your shopping list accordingly.
2. Pop out into the garden regularly (even if it's just to hang the washing out!) and take a second to check on your plants before you come back in.
3. Supermarket magazines often feature advice on using seasonal produce – some of which may be growing on your plot.
4. If you have a glut then pick a day when you have some spare time and harvest the lot for storage.
5. If you've got an unfamiliar vegetable, or a glut of something familiar, then do some research into new recipes to make use of them.
6. Don't let salad languish in the fridge. If you have more growing, it's fine to compost those sad-looking remnants – you don't have to eat them!
7. There are lots of recipe sites on the internet, many of which have tools to suggest recipes around your list of ingredients. The BBC Food website is a good place to start (www.bbc.co.uk/food).
8. Find some recipes that are nice cold or reheated, then make extra portions for use in packed lunches.
9. Making soups and smoothies is a quick way to make good use of lots of fresh fruit and vegetables.
10. It may be useful to hang a small blackboard in the kitchen, and make a note of which crops are ready, or almost ready, to harvest. That way everyone in the family knows what's coming.

♛ RECIPES BY SEASON ♛

SPRING

Although the garden comes to life in spring, and there's plenty of work for the gardener, it can be a lean time for the cook. Here are some ideas to make the most of the fresh new growth, and the last of the winter stores.

Seasonal highlights

- Add shredded spring cabbage to stir-fries, or lightly boil it to make bubble and squeak.

- Asparagus spears are at their best lightly boiled or steamed, then served with drizzled butter and a sprinkling of pepper, or Hollandaise sauce.

- Indulge your sweet tooth with a rhubarb crumble, or a deliciously tart rhubarb fool.

- The first broad beans of the season are traditionally paired with bacon — try combining them both in a spring risotto.

Use fresh

Broad bean mezze platter

Ingredients
(Serves 4)

227g ($\frac{1}{2}$ lb) of broad beans

227g ($\frac{1}{2}$ lb) of grated parmesan cheese (omit the cheese for a vegan version)

2 cloves of garlic, peeled

4 sprigs of basil, or mint

A splash of lemon juice

Salt and pepper to taste

Olive oil

1. Boil the broad beans until they're just tender, then drain and allow to cool. If your beans are mature you can gently pop them out of their skins, but it's not essential.

2. Put the beans, cheese (if using), garlic and herbs into a blender and blitz until smooth (or mostly smooth, if you prefer a chunky dip). Add lemon juice, salt and pepper to taste.

3. With the blender on its lowest setting, drizzle in olive oil until you're happy with the consistency. You can add a little water, too, if you're watching your waistline.

4. Chill for at least an hour before serving.

5. Serve in a bowl as the centrepiece of a large platter. Arrange raw vegetables (cauliflower florets and carrot sticks if in season) and toasted pitta quarters around the outside. You may find fresh parsley in the garden to use as a garnish.

This produces enough dip for four people, or more if used as part of a larger spread. It will keep in the fridge for a couple of days, and can also be served with jacket potatoes or potato wedges.

Stir-fried chard

Ingredients
(Serves 1)

2–3 chard leaves, or a small bunch of leaf beet, per person
Oil for frying (sunflower or vegetable)
1 clove of garlic, chopped
Ground ginger or five-spice seasoning
Soy sauce
Sesame oil

1. Wash your leaves thoroughly and shake dry. It doesn't matter if some spots of water remain.

2. If you're using chard then separate the leaves and stems. Roughly chop the stems. Cut the leaves into fat strips.

3. Heat a tablespoon or two of oil in a wok or large frying pan. Add the garlic – it should sizzle nicely, but not burn. Add the ground ginger or five-spice seasoning and stir for a minute or two before adding the chard stalks.

4. Stir-fry for a couple of minutes, until the chard stalks begin to soften, then add the chopped leaves.

5. Continue cooking for another couple of minutes, until the leaves have wilted. Stir in soy sauce, and a teaspoonful of sesame oil (or to taste), then serve over boiled rice or noodles.

You can omit the sesame oil if you don't have it, or don't like it. You can use black bean sauce, or oyster sauce, in place of soy sauce if you want a different flavour.

Pocket Tip 🛒

Stir-fried chard also makes a nice side dish served with chops or sausages.

COOK FROM STORES

With summer on the way, it's time to use up the last of your stored fruit and vegetables, and winter crops, in preparation for the new season.

Potato and leek soup

Ingredients
(Serves 4)

2 mature leeks, or a handful if smaller
Butter or oil for frying
1 onion, chopped
1 clove of garlic, peeled and chopped
400g ($\frac{3}{4}$ lb) potatoes, peeled and cut into chunks
Salt and pepper to taste
570ml (1 pint) water, chicken or vegetable stock
Cream (optional)
Chopped chives or parsley (to garnish)

1. Trim the leeks to remove the roots and the tough tops of the leaves. Slice (about the thickness of a pound coin is fine) and

then wash well to remove any traces of grit (it gets caught between the layers).

2. Heat a spoonful or two of oil (or a knob of butter) in a large saucepan and then fry the onion and garlic until they start to brown.

3. Add the potatoes and the leeks, then season with salt and pepper.

4. Cover with the water or stock, bring to the boil and then simmer until the vegetables are tender.

5. If you want a smooth soup you can allow it to cool slightly and blend it at this point.

6. If you want to add cream then stir it into the soup over a gentle heat, just before serving. Check the seasoning now, too.

7. Serve with a topping of chopped chives or parsley as a garnish.

You can omit the cream for the low-calorie version. Alternatively, serve with quartered slices of cheese on toast for a winter warmer version!

Roasted vegetables

This is an easy recipe to scale – simply provide one or two of each vegetable per person, depending on tastes, hunger levels and whether you're serving this as a main course or a side dish.

Ingredients

A selection of root vegetables (carrots, parsnips, swede, Jerusalem artichokes)
Onions
Olive oil
1 clove of garlic, chopped
Salt and pepper to taste

1. Preheat the oven to 200°C/400°F/gas mark 6.

2. Wash or peel all of the root vegetables, then cut them into bite-sized chunks.

3. Peel the onion and slice it into quarters.

4. Put all of the vegetables and the garlic into a large, lidded container with a couple of tablespoons of olive oil, then add salt and pepper. Put the lid on and shake! You can also use a bowl and stir to combine the ingredients, but make sure the vegetables are all coated in the oil.

5. Arrange the vegetables in a single layer on a baking tray or roasting tin. Use a slotted spoon if you've overdone the oil slightly – you don't want them swimming. Keep any spare oil for basting.

6. Roast for around an hour, stirring every 15 minutes. Add extra oil if the vegetables start sticking.

7. The dish is ready to serve when all of the vegetables are tender.

If you have any leftovers, they make a nice addition to vegetable soup.

Pocket Tip

In summer you can roast courgettes, tomatoes and aubergines for a Mediterranean version, but remember that they cook much more quickly than root vegetables.

SUMMER

Seasonal highlights

- You really haven't tasted peas until you've eaten them straight from the pod, while you're still standing in the garden!

- The first strawberries of the season are a treat on their own. Try sprinkling them with black pepper, rather than drowning them in cream, or throw a handful into your breakfast muesli.

- Dissolve a spoonful of sugar in warm rice wine vinegar, then pour over chopped cucumber. Sprinkle on chopped dill, season with salt and pepper, then leave in the fridge to marinate. Drain the liquid before serving and you have an instant pickle.

● Wander round the garden with a bowl and pick the youngest, freshest leaves from leafy green vegetables and herbs. Throw in a few edible flowers for a summery salad packed with flavour.

Use fresh

You may not feel like cooking in the heat of the summer, but these recipes are quick and easy ways to make the most of the fresh goodies coming in from the garden.

Minty potato salad

This recipe can be adjusted for any number; a large handful of new potatoes per person should suffice, but be warned – this dish is very moreish!

Ingredients

New potatoes, boiled and cooled
Bunch of mint leaves
Mayonnaise or crème fraîche

1. Chop the new potatoes into bite-sized chunks.

2. Roughly chop the mint leaves, to release their flavour.

3. Use a good dollop of mayonnaise or crème fraîche per person and combine all of the ingredients in a large bowl.

4. Can be served freshly made or prepared in advance and chilled.

Gazpacho

Ingredients
(Serves 4)

1kg (2lb) tomatoes
1 onion, or a bunch of spring onions
1 sweet pepper
1 small cucumber (or $\frac{1}{2}$ large one)

Fresh basil
Olive oil
Vinegar
Salt and pepper to taste

1. Roughly chop the tomatoes and the onion(s). Remove the seeds from the pepper and chop, then peel and chop the cucumber. Remove the basil leaves from the stalks, and discard the stalks.

2. Blend all the vegetables until smooth.

3. Pass the liquid through a sieve to remove any remaining chunks, tomato skin or seeds.

4. Rinse the blender and pour the sieved liquid back in. Blend on the lowest setting, while drizzling in oil and vinegar to taste.

5. Season with salt and pepper.

6. Serve chilled.

Pocket Tip 🖐

You can also make fruit soups by blending fruit with fruit juices. Chill before serving for a refreshing start to a meal.

COOK TO STORE

Make use of gluts now to bring a taste of summer to the long winter months.

Ratatouille

This freezes well for future use.

Ingredients
(Serves 4)

2 tomatoes
Olive oil for frying
1 onion, peeled and chopped

1 clove of garlic, peeled and chopped
1 aubergine, diced
1 courgette, diced,
1 sweet pepper, diced
Salt and pepper to taste

1. To peel the fresh tomatoes, cover them with boiling water and leave them for up to a minute, until the skins start to split. Plunge into cold water to cool, then peel off the skins.

2. De-seed and roughly chop your peeled tomatoes.

3. Heat the oil in a frying pan, then fry the onion and garlic over a low heat until they start to soften.

4. Add in the sweet pepper, courgette and aubergine and fry until softened.

5. Add the chopped tomatoes, then stir and heat through.

6. Season to taste.

7. Serve as a side dish for roast dinners, or as a pasta sauce.

If you don't like aubergines then simply replace them with another courgette; you're bound to have plenty!

Pocket Tip
If your aubergines are slightly bitter then slice and sprinkle with salt, then leave to stand for 15 minutes. Rinse and pat dry before cooking.

Lemon balm tea

This tea is made from five sprigs of fresh lemon balm per person, or a teaspoon of dried leaves. Simply steep the leaves in water that is just off the boil. Leave for at least five minutes.

Lemon balm makes a lovely winter tea as it soothes coughs and colds, so harvest the summer flush of leaves and dry them to store for the winter.

Pocket Tip 🛆

Mint tea is equally nice (and very good for your digestion), and plenty of other herbs make nice tea as well. Try mixing and matching to make your own perfect blend!

AUTUMN

Seasonal highlights

- You can cook sweetcorn in its papery husks on the barbecue, but you won't get the smoky flavour unless you remove them.

- A traditional Scottish cranachan dessert combines raspberries with whipped cream, honey and whisky, with a topping of toasted oatmeal.

- Courgette and squash flowers are delicious stuffed with cream cheese and deep-fried until crisp – and eating the flowers can help control a courgette glut!

- Thin strips of courgette can be used in place of pasta for a low-calorie meal. Simply blanch them for a minute and then combine them with a hot sauce.

Pocket Tip 🛆

Put the pan of water on to boil before you pick your sweetcorn cobs for the sweetest taste – their sugars start turning into starch as soon as they're picked.

Use fresh
Braised lettuce with peas

Cooking lettuce might sound batty, but this is a nice way to use up a glut.

Ingredients
(Serves 4)

4 small lettuces
Olive oil or butter for frying
1 onion, finely chopped
200ml ($\frac{1}{3}$ pint) chicken or vegetable stock
500g (about 1lb) shelled peas
4tbsp cream or crème fraîche

1. Remove any damaged outer leaves from the lettuces, and neatly trim the bottoms. Cut into halves or quarters (depending on size).

2. Gently fry the onion until it starts to soften.

3. Add the lettuce sections and fry for a minute, then flip and cook the other side.

4. Add the stock, put a lid on the pan and braise over a very low heat for 10 minutes.

5. Remove the lettuce with a slotted spoon and put to one side. Boil the liquid to reduce its volume by half, then add the peas and boil until tender.

6. Replace the lettuces in the pan, and stir in the cream or crème fraîche, if using.

7. Warm through and serve.

Simple sweetcorn chowder

Ingredients
(Serves 1)

145ml (5fl oz) cream
100g ($3\frac{1}{2}$ oz) new potatoes, cooked
White wine (optional)
$\frac{1}{2}$ corn on the cob, cooked
Salt and pepper to taste

1. Bring the cream to the boil in a small pan, then reduce the heat.

2. Add the potatoes and simmer for two to three minutes to warm the potatoes through.

3. Add a glug of white wine, if using, and simmer until the soup is of the desired consistency.

4. Meanwhile, use a knife to slice off the sweetcorn kernels, then add them to the pan. Heat through for a couple of minutes.

5. Season to taste.

COOK TO STORE

Strawberry jam

Ingredients
(This recipe fills around half a dozen jars)

1kg (2lb 3oz) fresh strawberries
1kg (2lb 3oz) sugar
Juice of $\frac{1}{2}$ lemon
A knob of butter

1. Put a saucer or small plate in the freezer to cool.

2. Remove the leaves and tough hulls from the strawberries, then cut them into halves.

3. Put the strawberries, sugar and lemon juice into a large saucepan.

4. Over a gentle heat, stir until the sugar is completely dissolved.

5. Boil hard. Every 10 minutes take the plate from the freezer and drip a little jam onto it. Wait a couple of seconds and then push the drop with your finger – if the surface wrinkles then the jam has reached its setting point and you're ready to move on. If it hasn't, keep boiling; expect it to need anything up to half an hour.

6. Turn off the heat and stir in the butter. Using a large spoon, skim off any scum that forms on the surface.

7. Allow to cool for 10 minutes, then pour into sterilised jam jars and put the lids on while the jam is still hot.

8. Label and store the jars once they have cooled.

Harvest chutney

Ingredients
(This recipe fills around half a dozen jars.)

680g ($1\frac{1}{2}$ lb) courgette, marrow or winter squash

680g ($1\frac{1}{2}$ lb) ripe tomatoes

680g ($1\frac{1}{2}$ lb) windfall (or cooking) apples

250g ($\frac{1}{2}$ lb) onions

250g ($\frac{1}{2}$ lb) raisins

250g ($\frac{1}{2}$ lb) brown sugar

375ml ($\frac{3}{4}$ pint) pale vinegar (eg white wine or cider)

200ml ($\frac{1}{2}$ pint) water

Fresh chilli (optional)

$\frac{1}{2}$ tsp salt

$\frac{1}{2}$ tsp ground ginger

1. Peel and roughly chop the fruit and vegetables.

2. Put all of the ingredients into a large pan. Heat gently and stir, to dissolve the sugar.

3. Bring to the boil, turn down the heat and simmer for about an hour. Stir occasionally to avoid it sticking. If necessary you can add a bit more water to stop the chutney drying out.

4. The chutney is finished when all of the ingredients are cooked and soft and it has the desired consistency.

5. Allow to cool for 10 minutes, then place into sterilised jars and put the lids on while still warm.

6. Label and store the jars once they have cooled.

WINTER

Seasonal highlights

- It's time to enjoy hearty baked potatoes – topped with anything from cheese and baked beans to smoked salmon and cream cheese.

- Baked apples are a deliciously healthy treat, topped with a little buttery syrup and raisins.

- Thin strips of cabbage make for a lovely, crunchy stir-fry, and pack a nutritious punch when added to winter soups.

- Try serving roast parsnips with a drizzle of maple syrup or honey.

Use fresh
Stuffed mushrooms

Ingredients
(Serves 1)

Butter or olive oil for frying
Tomatoes (fresh or tinned)
Kale, roughly chopped
2 large, flat mushrooms per person
Grated cheese
Salt and pepper

1. Preheat the oven to 180°C/350°F/gas mark 4.

2. Roughly chop the tomatoes, then heat them through gently in a pan with a little oil or butter.

3. In a separate pan, fry the kale until it starts to soften.

4. Put the mushrooms stem-side up on a baking tray. Cover with a layer of tomato, then one of kale. Top with a little grated cheese, then season to taste with salt and pepper (or use chilli flakes for a bit more heat).

5. Bake for 10 minutes or so, until the mushrooms are cooked through and the toppings are golden.

Chunky vegetable soup with dumplings

Ingredients
(Serves 4)

Oil for frying
1 onion, chopped
1 clove garlic, chopped
Pinch of dried mixed herbs

Selection of diced winter vegetables (potato, carrot, parsnip, leeks, celery, cabbage or kale)
850ml (1½ pint) vegetable or chicken stock
Salt and pepper

For the dumplings
2tbsp self-raising flour
1tbsp suet
Salt
Water

1. Fry the onion and garlic with the mixed herbs, until they start to soften.

2. Add the diced vegetables, then cover with the stock.

3. Season and bring to the boil. Cover and simmer for about half an hour, until all of the vegetables are tender.

4. Meanwhile, combine the flour and suet in a large mixing bowl with a pinch of salt. Slowly sit it in water until you form a thick mixture that you can form into balls with your hands.

5. Bring the soup to the boil again, then add the dumplings and simmer for 10 minutes until the dumplings are cooked through and fluffy.

COOK FROM STORES

Pea and mint soup

Ingredients
(Serves 4)

Large bunch of mint
1 litre (1¾ pints) water, chicken or vegetable stock
500g (about 1lb) frozen peas
Salt and pepper

1. Remove the mint leaves from the stalks, and discard the stalks.

2. Boil the liquid in a large saucepan, and add the mint leaves.

3. Add the peas, and boil for two to three minutes until the peas are just tender.

4. Strain the vegetables (reserving the liquid) and allow to cool slightly.

5. Blend the vegetables into a smooth paste, then add back in enough liquid to make a soup of the desired consistency.

6. Season to taste.

7. Serve hot in winter, or chill for a cooling summer treat.

Pocket Tip 🛒

This is a nice soup to make for kids, who generally like peas, as you can 'hide' leafy green vegetables like chard or spinach in it for an extra nutritional punch.

Homemade pizza

Ingredients

1 ready-made pizza base per person (or make your own)
Home-made tomato sauce or ratatouille (see p.153)
Grated cheese
Selection of toppings (sweetcorn, bacon, mushrooms, onion rings, extra cheese, ham, pineapple chunks)

1. Preheat the oven to 200°C/400°F/gas mark 6.

2. Spread a good layer of tomato sauce across your pizza base.

3. Sprinkle lightly with cheese.

4. Arrange your toppings.

5. Pop in the oven for 20–30 minutes, until the tomato sauce is bubbling and the cheese is starting to brown.

Pocket Tip 🛒

Don't forget to keep a note of your stores, and rotate them so that the oldest items are used first. That way they'll last longer, and you'll be ready for fresh supplies in spring.

INVOLVING CHILDREN

If you have kids then there are lots of good reasons to get them involved when you're gardening – they'll get exercise and fresh air, learn about natural cycles and wildlife and get hands-on experience of environmental issues, as well as other useful skills. Plus kids are more likely to want to eat fruit and vegetables they've grown themselves! In this chapter we look at fun things for kids to do on the allotment, as well as age-appropriate tasks. And we have some hints and tips on keeping the little ones safe.

♛ GARDENING TASKS ♛

Children often want to feel useful in the garden, or copy what you're doing. But growing plants can be tricky enough for adults, so it's important to give kids tasks that they can manage, and that have obvious results.

2–5 YEARS

- With a small watering can, or a bucket and a cup, even small children can have fun watering plants. This is an easy job that can be useful and is very hard to do wrong.

- Set aside a small area for your child to have their own 'garden' where they can dig holes, make mud pies, water weeds – whatever they love to do. A window box or a container on the patio is a good place to start if you have a smaller plot.

- Sowing big seeds such as beans, peas, onion sets, garlic cloves and potatoes is another good job if you don't mind wonky rows and aren't too worried about the final spacing.

- Putting things on the compost heap is easy, and a good opportunity to see what beasties have moved in.

- Harvesting is fun, although it needs to be supervised at this age. Peas, strawberries and salad leaves are all fun to munch while you're working on the plot.

Pocket Tip

Potatoes are a great source of 'buried treasure'. Help your child draw a map of where the seed potatoes are buried, so you can come back and dig up the treasure later in the year.

5–12 YEARS

- This is a good age for a child to have a proper patch where they can sow seeds and choose their own plants.

- Seed tapes and mats make sowing small and fiddly seeds easier, or sow salad crops that can be thinned for baby leaves.

- Sow fast-growing seeds, like cress, radishes and rocket, while you're waiting for bigger plants to grow.

- Older kids can give you a hand with the weeding, once you teach them how to recognise the difference between the plants and the weeds!

- They can also help you plant out herb plants you've bought, or strong seedlings you've grown at home.

- Raking leaves and making a leaf mould compost bin is a good job for the autumn.

Pocket Tip

Several seed companies have special ranges of seeds for children. Keep an eye out for the Fun to Grow range from Suttons and the Unwins Little Growers selection — both of which offer both flowers and vegetables.

13–16 YEARS

- Interest in gardening may wane as kids get older, but make them feel at home on the plot by putting up a hammock and bringing a barbecue.

- Teenagers can get involved with most gardening tasks, including digging and hoeing.

- Now even the smallest seeds won't give them any trouble – in fact they may be better at sowing the tiny ones than you are!

- If visits are becoming less regular, then your kid's plot is now better planted with things that can take care of themselves for longer, like potatoes and pumpkins, unless you're going to take care of the weeding yourself.

- Older children may be more interested in the allotment wildlife, or even sowing seeds to grow food for their own pets, than vegetable gardening for themselves.

Pocket Tip

JungleSeeds (www.jungleseeds.co.uk) has a selection of more unusual seeds that may appeal to older children and teenagers, and Seeds of Italy (www.seedsofitaly.com) has a range of seeds for pets.

♛ PROJECTS FOR CHILDREN ♛

Children aren't going to want to spend all of their time at the plot gardening, and they may want to 'garden' when you're not at the plot. Here are some fun garden-related ideas to try, on the allotment or at home.

Pocket Tip

The Secret Seed Society (www.secretseedsociety.com) is a children's gardening club with books, seeds and secret 'Seed Agent' missions.

FUN TASKS AT THE ALLOTMENT

- A selection of old clothes and a suitable stick can be turned into a scarecrow, with a little bit of straw for stuffing.

- Unwanted CDs can be strung together for a bird scarer.

- You can make a crawl tunnel fairly easily from tunnel hoops and mesh or a tarp.

- Leave a gap in your bean supports so that they form a wigwam, or even grow your own living-willow den.

- A bug viewer or a magnifying glass is all you need to go on a bug hunt.

- Seasonal ideas include an Easter egg hunt and decorating the plot for Halloween and Christmas.

- Putting up bird feeders, and keeping them filled, will bring in feathered friends. You could even make your own 'hide' for bird-watching.

Pocket Fact

Gardening for children is a hot topic – a new gardening show for children, Mr Bloom's Nursery, *started airing on CBeebies in February 2011.*

ARTS AND CRAFTS

- Making paper pots for seedlings is a fun way to while away a rainy afternoon. You can search for origami designs on the internet, or invest in a Paper Potter which makes the job very easy. Then all you need is scrap paper.

- If you're going to be saving your own seeds then try designing your own seed envelopes to keep them in!

- Plastic bottles can be turned into bird feeders, mini-cloches and homes for hibernating ladybirds and lacewings.

- Make your own windmills to decorate the plot.

- Keep an allotment scrapbook with pictures of your plants, dried leaves and flowers, and notes on how well your plants are growing.

- Paint wooden plant labels, or stones, for marking the rows.

- Painted signs are always nice on allotments, whether it's a simple number to identify your plot or a fancy name plate for the shed.

- Seeds collected from the plot can be used in mosaics.

- Look for interesting items to recycle as plant pots for the plot – maybe you've grown out of your wellies?

Pocket Tip 🖎

For more fun projects, have a look at the Royal Horticultural Society and BBC websites on gardening with children (www.rhs.org.uk/ children and www.bbc.co.uk/gardening/gardening_with_children).

♛ FUN PLANTS ♛

Adults may find plants fascinating, or merely useful, but to really engage in gardening children need to find them fun.

NURSERY RHYMES AND FAIRY TALES

Fruits and vegetables often feature in nursery rhymes, fairy tales and more modern children's stories. Try helping your child to grow along with their favourite stories.

- It's not as instant as Jack's magic beans, but you can grow your own beanstalk if you choose a tall, climbing bean variety. And you can save your own magic beans to grow again next year.

- Who grew the peas in the *Princess and the Pea*?

- Grow a giant pumpkin for Cinderella, and carve it into a carriage for Halloween.

- What did Peter Piper pick?

- Or Peter, Peter, Pumpkin eater?

CHILDREN'S FAVOURITES

- Radishes grow so quickly that they're great for young children who can't wait long to see some action.

- When bean seeds germinate they put on a good show, so sow some on the windowsill to plant out at the plot later.

- A pumpkin or two for Halloween is fun, and if you scratch your name into the skin it will grow with the pumpkin.

- Peas are irresistible, as they're so sweet straight out of the shell.

- Cress seeds can be grown anywhere, so try growing them in eggshells with faces on them to grow your own eggheads!

- Giant sunflowers are a perennial favourite, easy to grow, and great fun to measure – especially if you're having a race!

- Peanuts have an interesting trick up their sleeve: they bury their nuts underground. You'll need to find unshelled nuts in the pet or health store, then crack them open when you're ready to sow them. They're best grown on the windowsill, or in a greenhouse.

- Popcorn is grown the same way as sweetcorn, then dried on the cob for popping later.

- Cherry tomatoes are easily grown, and often too tempting to make it home from the plot!

Pocket Tip

The Natural History Museum shop has a great selection of gardening kits for kids – you could hatch your own butterflies to release in the garden, or have a space-age garden on the windowsill. You can also grow your plants in reindeer, elephant or rhino poo!

IMAGINATIVE PLANTS

Plants can have really dull names, but if you dream up your own then the possibilities are endless.

- Carnivorous plants are fun – Venus fly-traps and pitcher plants are great for ghoulish kids who would enjoy their own flesh-eating landscape. They can also help with pest control on the kitchen windowsill or in the greenhouse!

- Paracress (*Spilanthes oleracea*) is an annual herb in this country, with spectacular flowers that look like alien eyeballs on stalks! It's added to salads in small amounts and is also known as the toothache plant because it used to be used as a cure. It creates an interesting fizzy tingling sensation in the mouth.

- Try growing your own flying saucers, with patty-pan shaped summer squash.

- Grow your own edible 'fairy lanterns' with cape gooseberries (also known as physalis), which are grown like tomatoes (but avoid the ornamental Chinese lanterns, which are not edible).

- 'Mouse melons' (*Melothria scabra*) make a great lunchbox snack as they're like tiny cucumbers.

- And you can even grow your own eggs – if you choose an aubergine variety with small, white fruits!

Pocket Fact
The strawberry is the only fruit to have its seeds on the outside.

♛ HEALTH AND SAFETY ♛

There are hazards on the allotment for young and old alike. See p.60 for general healthy and safety information, but here are some tips for keeping the youngsters safe and sound.

TASKS TO AVOID

- Children should not be involved in the application of garden chemicals, and it is safest if they stay at home while chemicals are being applied.

- Don't let children use power tools, or sharp tools (secateurs and pruners) without adequate supervision.

- Bonfires and barbecues must be supervised by an adult at all times, and you should have water on hand to put the fire out if it starts to spark or get out of control.

PRECAUTIONS

- If you have a pond or a water butt then make sure it's covered over so that young children can't fall in.

- Use cane toppers on the tops of your canes and plant supports so there are no sharp points at the eye level of adults or children.

- Keep garden chemicals (organic or not) out of the reach of children.

- If you don't garden organically then make sure that the watering can or sprayer you use for chemicals is out of reach as well.

- Don't leave children unsupervised on the allotment and try to keep them from wandering onto other plots that may contain hazards.

- Make sure children have their own gloves, and sturdy shoes or boots.

- Be sun safe: keep children's skin covered and use plenty of sun block. A hat is essential, and make sure you have plenty of drinking water on hand in the summer.

Pocket Tip

Consider putting up a tipi, play house or a den so that children have a place to play and sit in the shade.

GLOSSARY

♛ COMMON GARDENING TERMS ♛

Allotment	A rented patch of ground used for growing food.
Annual	A plant that completes its lifecycle in one year.
Aspect	The way in which a plot faces.
Baby	A vegetable variety grown for small or 'baby' vegetables.
Biennial	A plant that completes its lifecycle in two years.
Bolting	Prematurely flowering and setting seed.
Bulbs	An underground crop, such as onions and garlic.
Catch-cropping	Planting a quick-growing crop (such as lettuce or radishes) before planting your main crop.
Chitting	Allowing potatoes to start sprouting before planting.
Clamp	An outdoor root store, made from earth and straw.
Community gardens	Outdoor spaces run by the community for gardening and recreation.
Community Supported Agriculture	Farms which are supported by the local community financially or with gardening help.

Companion planting
Growing different plants together, to benefit both (eg growing marigolds with tomatoes to discourage whitefly).

Compost
The finished product when organic matter is allowed to rot down.

Corm
The underground part of certain plants, including saffron, which is used for propagation.

Cut-and-come-again
Salad crops that are cut several times while leaving the plant in the ground, rather than lifted all at once.

Cutting
A way of propagating plants by rooting small sections of stem or root.

Division
Propagating a mature perennial plant by pulling or cutting it into smaller sections.

Double digging
A thorough method of soil preparation that involves digging to twice the normal depth.

Early
A plant variety that crops early in the season.

Earthing up
Mounding soil or compost around plant stems; most often done to protect potato tubers from sunlight.

F1 hybrid
A cross between two different plants that have specific characteristics (eg uniformity, vigour, disease resistance), resulting in plants that are very uniform.

Fertiliser
Plant food.

Frost
When the air or soil temperature drops below freezing. Damaging to tender plants.

Frost pocket
An area of the allotment that catches and holds frost.

Full sun An area with no shade.

Garden chemicals Pesticides, herbicides and fertilisers made from synthetic chemicals.

Germination A seed's first stage of growth.

Green manure A crop sown primarily to benefit the soil.

Guerrilla gardening Gardening on land you do not own or rent.

Hardy Plants that are not damaged by frost.

Herbs Plants primarily used as flavourings or medicinally.

Inbreeders Easy plants to save seed from as they are self-pollinating.

Intercropping Allowing two crops to share the same space.

Layering Propagating a plant by allowing a stem to root.

Maincrop Used to describe plant varieties that grow during the main growing season (as opposed to 'early' or 'late') or which make up the bulk of the harvest.

Manure Animal by-products used as fertiliser (*compare with* Green manure).

Mediterranean Plants that like a warm, sunny and dry climate.

Microclimates The different growing conditions in various areas within one garden or allotment.

Mulch A layer that covers the soil and prevents weeds. A mulch can be organic (eg bark chips, compost, cardboard) or made from plastic.

No dig	A method of gardening that involves as little soil disturbance as possible.
Organic	Gardening without the use of synthetic chemicals.
Ornamental	A plant primarily used for its decorative effect.
Outbreeders	Plants that cross-pollinate and are more difficult to save seed from.
Overwintering	Crops that grow through the winter.
Partial shade	An area that is not in full sun all day, due to shade cast by buildings or trees.
Perennial	A plant that lives for several years.
pH	Whether soil is acid or alkaline.
Plant families	Related plants are grouped into families, and families are moved together in a crop rotation.
Pollination	The process of transferring pollen from a male plant or flower to a female one, which leads to the production of seeds.
Potting on	Transfering a plant to a larger pot.
Propagation	Raising new plants, either by sowing seeds or using vegetative propagation.
Raised bed	A raised area of soil which is accessed from a path.
Rods	The esoteric unit of measurement used for allotments, which equals just over 5m (16 feet).
Rotation	Moving related crops around the plot to prevent the build-up of pests and disease.
Seed tape/mats	Seeds embedded in a tape or a mat, which are easier to sow.
Seedling	A young plant, grown from seed.

Self-fertile	A plant (or variety) with flowers that pollinate themselves.
Soft fruit	Fruit grown on bushes, eg strawberries, blackberries and raspberries.
Successional	Sowing or planting the same crop at intervals, to ensure a continuous supply.
Sundries	Useful items that are not tools, eg string and plant labels.
Tender	Plants that are damaged by frost.
Tilth	Soil texture.
Tree fruit	Fruit grown on trees, eg apples and pears.
Undercropping	Planting a low-growing crop under a taller one.
Vegetative propagation	Growing new plants from parts of existing plants (eg through taking cuttings, division or layering).
Weeds	Unwanted plants, although they may be useful.
Wind rock	When strong winds rock a tall plant and dislodge its roots.

♛ USEFUL EQUIPMENT ♛

Cane toppers	Plastic or rubber covers that prevent you from poking your eye when you bend over garden canes.
Canes	Sticks used to support plants.
Cloche	A smallish plant cover, used to protect plants from weather or pests.
Cold frame	An unheated frame with a glass lid, which protects plants.
Compost bin	A specific area or bin for making compost.

Dibber	A device for making holes for sowing and planting.
Fleece	A breathable fabric used for crop protection.
Forcing pot	Used to encourage early spring crops (eg rhubarb) that are also starved of light ('blanched').
Fork	A large fork is used for digging; a hand fork mostly for weeding.
Garden line	A string with two ends that can be pushed into the ground to guide sowing and planting into straight lines.
Gloves	Protection for hands.
Greenhouse	A structure made largely from glass or clear plastic which is used for plant protection.
Hoe	Used for weeding.
Knee pads	Used to protect your knees when kneeling.
Knife	A garden knife is used for cutting twine and harvesting.
Lights	Essentially windows; the clear lids of cold frames.
Polytunnel	A large, clear plastic tunnel used for crop protection.
Rake	Used for clearing leaves or smoothing the soil surface.
Riddle	A garden sieve, used for taking the lumps out of compost.
Rotavator	A mechanical digger.
Secateurs	Garden scissors.
Seed trays	Shallow trays used for sowing seeds.
Shears	Large garden scissors.

Spade	Used for digging.
Trowel	Used for planting and harvesting.
Trug	A traditional shallow basket with a handle, used for harvesting.
Tunnel	Low plastic or mesh tunnels are used for crop protection.
Twine	Garden string (natural or plastic).
Water butt	A container for storing rain water.
Watering can	Used for watering plants by hand.
Wheelbarrow	Good for moving large quantities of things around the allotment.

GROWING CALENDAR

The growing calendar below shows you when you should be sowing, planting out and harvesting your crops (see Chapter 6 for more detailed information on each crop).

There's also some space at the end to add in some of your own crops, as a handy reminder. The growing calendar is divided into spring, summer, autumn and winter, and then into months.

Remember that the months are more of a guideline though, as spring will arrive at different times depending on where you are! There can be as much as eight weeks difference between when spring arrives, from the south of England to the north of Scotland. The further north you are, the shorter the spring/summer growing season will be, and the more you will need to focus on hardy fruits and vegetables. Late frosts, in spring, are more likely if you live inland than on the coast.

Pocket Tip 🛞

Keep an eye on the weather forecast in spring and autumn; if frost is forecast you can bring tender plants under cover, or harvest crops safely.

KEY

S = Sow seeds

P = Plant out plants or seedlings

H = Harvest

CROP	SPRING			SUMMER				AUTUMN			WINTER	
	March	April	May	June	July	August	September	October	November	December	January	February
Asparagus	P	SP	SH	H								
Aubergines	S		P	P		H	H					S
Basil	S		SP	PH	H	H	H					
Beetroot		S	S	SH	SH	H	H					
Beans (broad)				H	H				S			S
Beans (French)	S	S	SP	SPH	SPH	PH	H					
Broccoli (sprouting)	S	SH	SH	P								S
Broccoli (summer)		S	S	SH	H	H	H	H				
Cabbage (spring)		H	H		S	S	P	P				
Cabbage (summer)	SP	SP	PH	H								
Cabbage (autumn)		S			P	P		H	H	H		S
Cabbage (winter)			S	SP	P					H	H	H
Calabrese		S	SP	H	H	H						
Carrots	S	SH	SH	SH	SH	H	H					S

Cauliflower (summer)	SP	P	P		SP	H	H				S	S
Cauliflower (winter)		S	SH	SH		P	P	P				
Celeriac	SH		P	P			H	H	H	H	H	SH
Celery	S		P	P		H	H	H	SH	H		S
Chard	SH	SH	SPH	PH	H	H	SPH	SH				
Courgettes		S	SP	P	H	H	H					
Cucumbers		S	P	PH	H	H	H					
Garlic				H	H				P			
Globe artichokes	S		P		H	H						S
Jerusalem artichokes	P								H	H	P	P
Kale	H	S	S	P	P			H	H	H	H	H
Leeks	SH	SH	SH	P	P		H	H	H	H	H	H
Salad leaves	S	S	SPH	SPH	SPH	SPH	SPH	SPH	H	H	H	SH
Onions (maincrop)	SP	SP		H	H	H						
Onions (Japanese)				H	SH	S	SP	P				

CROP	SPRING			SUMMER			AUTUMN			WINTER		
	March	April	May	June	July	August	September	October	November	December	January	February
Parsley	S	SP	SPH	PH	PH	SH	SPH	H	H	H		
Parsnips	SH	S	S					H	H	H	H	SH
Peas	S	S	S	SH	H	H	H	S	S			
Peppers	S		P	P	H	H	H					S
Potatoes		P	P	H	H	H	H					
Radishes	SH	SH	SH	SH	SH	SH	SH	H				S
Sweetcorn		S	SP			H	H	H				
Tomatoes			P	P	H	H	H					S
Winter squashes		S	SP	P			H					

MY CROPS

CROP	SPRING			SUMMER			AUTUMN			WINTER		
	March	April	May	June	July	August	September	October	November	December	January	February